The Concept of Philosophy

THE CONCEPT
OF PHILOSOPHY

R. W. NEWELL
Lecturer in Philosophy
The University of East Anglia

METHUEN & CO LTD

distributed in the United States
by BARNES & NOBLE, Inc.

First published 1967 by Methuen & Co Ltd
© 1967 by R. W. Newell
Printed in Great Britain by
Butler and Tanner Ltd,
Frome and London

Contents

Preface

Kant asked how metaphysics is possible, and answered that it is knowledge *a priori*, or out of pure understanding and pure reason. He noticed too that there is nothing in this to distinguish metaphysics from pure mathematics. The problem of the nature of metaphysical – or philosophical – knowledge is at the centre of this book. The problem is one of reconciling the reflective nature of philosophical reasoning with its non-deductive character while retaining the possibility of philosophical knowledge.

The views put forward in this book derive from the work of Professor John Wisdom. I have received much valuable assistance from his lectures on proof and explanation, and perhaps the full extent of my debt will be appreciated only by those who have closely followed his work. I do not expect that he would agree with all the arguments or tolerate the mistakes that remain. I am also indebted to Mr J. R. Bambrough of St John's College, Cambridge, for helpful advice on a number of topics.

R. W. NEWELL

I

Some Dogmas of Philosophy

1. *Foreword*

In these pages my purpose is to outline the parts and operations of an influential doctrine about the nature and limitations of reasoning. This doctrine is sometimes wielded as a pioneer axe in the destruction of metaphysical thickets, clearing the ground for the proper work of philosophy. Or else it may no less effectively operate behind the scenes in a philosopher's theorizing, making its appearance in its consequences rather than in its canons. Its fundamental narrative is simple and has the attractiveness of a portable philosophical manœuvre of wide application. Most philosophers have at some time felt the pinch of its restricting ordinances as well as gratification at its quick disposal of humbug and muddle. Many have unreflectingly incorporated its vital parts in their own intellectual conduct, and remain unaware how much of the source of their philosophical puzzlement resides in these adopted habits of thought. In this book it will not be argued that the dogmas of the doctrine need to be revised. They are beyond revision, and are one great mistake.

In a loose sense this body of theory comes from Hume, or from interpreters of Hume, and the specific *locus* is his division of reasoning into the distinct departments of 'relations of ideas' and 'matters of fact'. We recognize on the one hand reasoning by logical or mathematical demonstration, and on the other reasoning based on the promise of past and the prospect of future observations. The doctrine charted here allows no further room for reason. It is the view that a respectable argument must present the credentials of deduction if it cannot be justified in the light of additional observation.

Its central thesis is that reasoning which is neither inductive nor deductive cannot be reasoning at all since the means of proving,

confirming or justifying a proposition is vested only in these two procedures. In the most traditional form of the dogma, deduction is held
to be a paradigm of justification, although the absurdity of this is sometimes recognized and induction is admitted as an equal partner with a
different job of its own. One notorious consequence of this division of
labour is that argument conducted by any other practice is always
dubious, and the results of that argument always doubtful. This feature
alone is a major source of philosophical perplexity.

It is worth looking at some of the corollaries. Relations between
reasons and conclusions, or between concepts and their characteristics,
are restricted to causal or logically necessary connections. The bug-
bear of this thesis is the idea of a non-necessary *a priori* relation. It is a
consequence, too, that *a priori* reasoning has no bearing on matters of
fact, and what is logically possible has no effect on what actually
happens. To reason *a priori* is to reason deductively, and to do this is
not to turn up any new information in any new conclusions. It is to
repeat, laboriously, what one already knows. On the other side, a
question is a question of fact only if it calls for further empirical investigation; otherwise it is a question of logic to be settled by a demonstration. And if all the investigations and demonstrations have been
done, then it is a question of neither sort and no answer to it could be
true or false; perhaps it is not a question at all. Reason, in this case,
'has no further room to operate'.

The theory contained in this doctrine carries, on a grand scale, a
specially persistent puzzle into every department of philosophy. It
occurs whenever reasons are given for answers, or premises are given
for conclusions. There are premises about sensations, conclusions about
material things; premises about behaviour, conclusions about mind;
premises about matters of fact, conclusions about matters of value;
premises about the present, conclusions about the past; no doubt the
list could be extended. In each case the traditional strategy is to ask
whether the connection between premise and conclusion is contingent
or logically necessary, and then to point out that any answer given to
this question is unsatisfactory. For if the connection is said to be contingent, it will be shown to be unverifiable, and if it is said to be
necessary it will be shown to be invalid. If it is said to be neither, it will
be argued that there is no connection since these are the only two there

could be. The traditional counter-strategy is to deny that the connection is contingent, or to deny that it is necessary, but not to deny that it must be of one or the other kind. The argument leads directly to scepticism by systematically undercutting any hope of justifying the conclusions or answers by acceptable inference from the premises or reasons.

If these dogmas influence the course of philosophical disputes about the nature of non-philosophical inquiries, they equally influence the course of philosophical disputes about the nature of philosophical inquiries. Philosophical argument itself is an especially vulnerable target for anyone using these weapons. In a moment we shall take up some of the standard manœuvres and stock responses when this doctrine is deployed against philosophical reasoning. They are not very different from the manœuvring and responding that occurs whenever it is deployed.

It is probably untrue that Hume is the author of all, or even most, of these dogmas. Yet it is no accident that philosophers who have expounded them have closely associated their work with his, in spirit if not in print. The elements are there in the *Treatise* and the *Enquiry*, and remain in the development of empiricist philosophy from his time to ours. Needless to say, bits of these dogmas are comfortably housed in Locke and Berkeley. However, I am conscious that there seems to be something of the shape of a straw man about this unrefined doctrine; no one, it will be said, does put things in *exactly* this way. Well, it does not matter much. The intention is less to point a finger at an accused than to indicate the environment and character of the misdemeanour. One way to see these dogmas for what they are is to present them nakedly, even crudely, brushing aside the caution and qualification which gains in documentation what it loses in insight. And insight into the bare mechanics of philosophical argument is needed.

To return to Hume. In Appendix I of the *Enquiry* he gives an argument that has extensive repercussions and is, possibly, the keystone of the philosophical monument adumbrated here. He raises the issue mainly in connection with his views on moral philosophy, and the position is this. In any situation in which all the required observations have been done, and all the relevant data are known, and also when any required calculations and deductions have been completed, it is pointless to debate that situation further. Additional 'reasoning' about the matter is not real reasoning; continuing disagreement is not real disagreement:

> But in moral deliberations we must be acquainted beforehand with all the objects, and all their relations to each other . . . No new fact to be ascertained; no new relation to be discovered. All the circumstances of the case are supposed to be laid before us, ere we can fix any sentence of blame or approbation . . . But after every circumstance, every relation is known, the understanding has no further room to operate, nor any object on which it could employ itself . . . Nothing remains but to feel, on our part, some sentiment of blame or approbation . . .

The immediate intention of the argument is to show that moral arguments do not concern themselves with matters of fact, that they are not *arguments* in any proper sense; there is no way of establishing or of refuting the conclusions of rival parties in a moral dispute once observations, and perhaps demonstrations, fail to decide the issue. The issues are undecidable because they cannot be decided by either of the two standard procedures and they are, therefore, no more than conflicts of the sentiments.

The scope of the argument is much wider than Hume's limited employment of it in ethics. Here seems to be a piece of reasoning effectively discrediting *any* questions or disputes that continue beyond a point where observation and demonstration stop. If it applies to moral deliberations it applies equally and in the same way to philosophical deliberations. Rival philosophers agree about the empirical facts, and agree that there is no need for further deductions from these facts, yet continue to debate a philosophical point. According to Hume's argument, so far from being substantial their disagreement is, in default, not a rational or settleable disagreement at all. Of course, there are two kinds of dispute against which this argument is wholly ineffective and these are disputes that can be settled by further investigation or by logical demonstration.

Most of the dogmas outlined here underlie, with different degrees of emphasis, three chief theories about the nature and place of philosophical reasoning: Hume's own theory, logical positivism, and a number of interconnected accounts of the function of philosophical discourse known as the 'verbal recommendations' thesis. Some thumbnail sketches will show that each of them reaches its conclusions about the nature of philosophy as a consequence of an overt or implicit allegiance to the main features of this traditional doctrine.

2. *Hume*

Hume's *Treatise* is an intensive criticism of a particular method of philosophizing, and he reprimands his opponents for their general conception of philosophy as much as for their answers to standing philosophical questions. His own constructive views are revealed by the sub-title, 'An Attempt to introduce the experimental Method of Reasoning into Moral Subjects'. For Hume, philosophy is an empirical study of the nature of human reasoning. Representing his own work as a 'science of man', he undertakes to chart the 'mental geography, or delineations of the distinct parts and powers of the mind', and to 'anatomize human nature in a regular manner', all of which he reckons 'must be based on experience and observation'. 'This author', he writes of himself in the *Abstract*, 'promises to draw no conclusions but where authorized by experience.' A philosophical inquiry is a special kind of empirical study having the 'peculiar disadvantage' of not being subject to experimental control, but of appealing to facts 'as they appear in the common course of the world'. Hume presents us with, as he thinks, a documentary album.

His programme is a sustained assault on the rationalist conception of philosophy, that 'unclear and chimerical' *a priori* theorizing about matters of fact. And it is this spurious metaphysical pursuit which he commits to the flames, after explaining his reason: it contains neither 'abstract reasoning concerning quantity or number' nor 'experimental reasoning concerning matters of fact and existence'. Lacking these qualifications, it can contain only sophistry and illusion. At least this is his belief.

Hume's belief that the proper conduct of philosophical method is descriptive and empirical, from which he never wavers, is partly the product of a misconception that he shares with his rationalist opponents, despite his rejection of their thesis. Let us agree that Hume has exposed error and confusion in attempts to establish propositions about the physical world solely by demonstration from *a priori* principles. But notice that he was arguing against an opposition sharing with him the belief that the object of philosophical investigation is to provide information about matters of fact and existence. Neither Hume nor the rationalists dispute the point that philosophy is properly an investigation of material and mental phenomena. The contention is about the method by which this investigation is to be conducted. Hume wishes to introduce the 'experimental method' against his opponents' *a priori* procedure. The strength of Hume's critique does not lie in his opposition to philosophy regarded as an *a priori* study, but in his claim that rationalism uses *a priori* methods in such a way as to guarantee their failure. If philosophy is an investigation of empirical phenomena then the rationalist programme must be abandoned. But the thesis that the proper object of philosophy is the study of common and not-so-common matters of fact can still be questioned, even though, *if* this is the object, Hume's methods are appropriate. In the course of this book it will be argued, against Hume, that philosophy is in no sense a department of science. It is, on the contrary, an *a priori* investigation. This does not mean, as might be thought, that we must thereby regard philosophical reasoning as a species of demonstrative argument. For this is to fall into the theoretical trap unsuccessfully avoided by Hume and two theories shortly to be inspected.

Hume was not the last philosopher to find that metaphysics can be destroyed only at the price of a dilemma. It may reasonably be asked whether he is bound to follow his opponents into the flames. Obviously Hume believed he had the qualifications for survival by regarding philosophy as an empirical, and so legitimate, investigation. Interestingly enough his confidence was never shaken by the paradoxical fact that his own philosophical arguments, not being deductive, are also not authorized by experience in the way he supposed. The examples which he has 'judiciously collected and compared' are not restricted to the records of actual events and documentary happenings. Hume failed to see that his arguments are based on the possibility of an example rather than on its actual occurrence. And this is easy to overlook, for if a case actually happened then it logically could have happened, but if it could have happened it does not follow that it ever would have, will or did. Hume's assumption was to suppose that by citing an instance of an actual occurrence to support a possibility of logic, he was not doing something markedly different from one who cites an actual instance to support a possibility of fact. If the second technique is scientific, or nearly so, the first is not. The truth is that fictional cases would have served him as well as the actual ones (presuming they are actual) which he presented. For example, in his exposition of causal connections there would be no loss to the force or logic of his argument if he had argued from a case where, let us say, every time a person mixes hot water with cold a red liquid results. That this is not what actually happens is irrelevant to the philosophical discovery drawn from it; it is logically comparable to his case of the observed billiard balls, but no evidence for a contingent conclusion. It begins to look as though Hume, by bringing philosophy within one of the two respectable provinces of reasoning, has not so easily escaped the fate of metaphysicians.

In the *Tractatus* Wittgenstein, like Hume, insisted that metaphysical statements are senseless; significant propositions assert matters of fact, and all other propositions, apart from tautologies, have no meaning. Thus the door is closed to metaphysics in an uncomfortable Humean way. But Wittgenstein, unequivocal in his pronouncement that 'philosophy is not one of the natural sciences', does not take advantage of Hume's exit and identify philosophy with an empirical study. Nor does he follow the route of his positivist successors and rescue his arguments by endowing them with logical necessity. His paradoxical if somewhat heroic action is straightforwardly to admit that his own philosophical remarks must be nonsensical. Nevertheless Wittgenstein points, though no more than points, to a way out, by proposing that philosophy is an activity of clarification with the job of thinning the ranks of discourse by eliminating meaningless propositions. Yet he adds that this activity is not a theory, or a doctrine, and retains the belief that its statements are, in their own right, senseless. Rather than resolve the dilemma of the elimination of metaphysics Wittgenstein let it stand. If philosophy is nonsensical it remains, in Ramsey's phrase, 'important nonsense'.

3. *Logical positivism*

In the first number of *Erkenntnis* Carnap writes a manifesto of a new method of philosophizing, to be distinguished sharply from traditional procedures:

> Thus, philosophy is no longer viewed as a domain of knowledge in its own right, on a par with, or superior to, the empirical sciences ... Logic is no longer one philosophical discipline among others, but we are able to say outright: Logic is the method of philosophizing.[1]

The arguments supporting this slogan turn out to be the positivist version of Hume's dichotomy, one even more clear-cut and decisive than Hume's own statement. Significant or meaningful propositions are divided into two classes, formal propositions of logic expressing tautologies, and factual propositions which are empirically verifiable. The division is supposed to be exhaustive. Hume's indictment is 'but a rhetorical version of our own thesis that a sentence which does not express either a formally true proposition or an empirical hypothesis is devoid of literal significance'.[2] Given this classification and the claim that metaphysical propositions are neither logically true nor empirically testable, the elimination of metaphysics follows as a matter of course. Yet a problem remains:

> But what, then, is left over for *philosophy*, if all statements whatever that assert something are of an empirical nature and belong to factual science? What remains is not statements, nor a theory, nor a system, but only a *method*: the method of logical analysis.[3]

This is a clear departure from Hume. His solution of identifying philosophy with an empirical investigation is held to be inadmissible; according to positivism science is science and nothing else, and philosophy, being *a priori*, forfeits any claim to be a science. Nor will Wittgenstein's solution in the *Tractatus* do either, it is too equivocal and paradoxical: 'After all,' Russell remarks, 'Mr Wittgenstein

---

[1] 'The Old and the New Logic', *Logical Positivism*, ed. A. J. Ayer, London 1959, p. 133.
[2] A. J. Ayer, *Language, Truth and Logic*, second edition, London 1946, p. 54.
[3] Carnap, 'The Elimination of Metaphysics', *Logical Positivism*, p. 77.

manages to say a good deal about what cannot be said.' In fact, there is no choice of what course to take, given the theoretical conditions of the courses possible:

> The propositions of philosophy are not factual, but linguistic in character ... they express definitions, or the formal consequences of definitions. Accordingly, we may say that philosophy is a department of logic. For the characteristic mark of a purely logical enquiry is that it is concerned with the formal consequences of our definitions and not with questions of empirical fact.[1]

The thesis is that every philosophical question can be settled once and for all by a demonstrative analysis; the proper activity of philosophy is conducted by formulating definitions and deducing sets of logical equivalences. Confining himself to analysis of this kind, a philosopher escapes metaphysics on the one hand and science on the other, avoiding as well Wittgenstein's untenable answer.

The archetypal method of philosophizing, and as it turns out the only working example of an analysis, is Russell's theory of descriptions. Basically a straightforward if at first unobvious deduction of one statement from another, it has the attractive feature that descriptive phrases which occur in the sentence to be analysed are eliminated in the equivalent translation. Partly because deductive analysis along the lines of the theory of descriptions did overcome philosophical puzzlement in some special cases, it was taken as a 'paradigm of philosophy' to dispatch puzzlement in all cases.[2] What would be more plausible than to suppose that analysis of a similar kind is the key to other and more important solutions? For one thing, it seems to provide a method of solving the philosophical problem of perception by demonstrating that statements about material things are logically reducible to sets of statements which mention no material things. The proposed reduction

[1] *Language, Truth and Logic*, p. 57.

[2] Russell's translations solved a problem by removing the puzzlement a person is likely to have from wondering whether there is a sense in which the things that we know never existed do exist. The philosophical problems his translations were borrowed to solve are altogether different; in this case, the translations attempt to remove the puzzlement a person is likely to have from wondering whether there is a sense in which the things that we know do exist do not. None of them have ever succeeded. None could.

is an essential part in the mechanism of positivist espitemology: in order to sustain the leading principle that every significant, non-tautologous statement is empirically verifiable, it is necessary to explain the relationship between statements about the material world and statements expressing the immediate observations which provide the final basis of verification. The relationship is held to be logically necessary and the task of producing a translation becomes the chief issue.

While the separation of 'philosophy' as a branch of logic and 'metaphysics' as a meaningless occupation is a direct consequence of the rigid empirical-analytic division, this anti-metaphysical move gains further support by way of a special explanation of the origins of metaphysical statements. If metaphysics is meaningless, why has it ever been practised? The answer is ingenious. Metaphysics arises because of a particular sort of mistake unwittingly made by its practitioners since a metaphysician has strung together a nonsensical group of words in a grammatically correct way, supposing, and this is his mistake, that a sentence expresses a meaningful proposition simply because it has the grammatical appearance of a meaningful sentence. His failure is to see that it does not express any proposition at all. Once again, Hume's division is the silent partner in the operation.

4. The 'verbal recommendations' concept

This theory of the nature of philosophical and metaphysical statements is best introduced by considering a question which played a central role in its development: Can two persons dispute about a matter of fact if each person knows all the facts needed to resolve the issue? In 'Metaphysics and Verification' John Wisdom presents a case to illustrate the question. 'If when a dog attacks her, a cow keeps her horns always towards him, so that she rotates as fast as he revolves, does he go round her?'; we may imagine observers reasoning 'He does go round her because he encircles her' or 'He does not go round her because he never gets behind her'.[1] Wisdom himself is less interested in the answers which his imaginary disputants might give than in the nature of the argument which ensues between them. On the face of it

---

[1] *Philosophy and Psycho-Analysis*, Oxford 1957, pp. 95–7.

the question they debate is a question of fact, whether the dog went round the cow, but the example contains a special and philosophically interesting feature. Nothing in the situation is hidden from any of the observers and there is no question of a need to make further empirical investigations, presuming the disputing persons have each seen enough. By watching further they would not see anything they had not seen already. Yet the argument does not, as might be expected, come to an agreed conclusion. Are they disputing a question of fact?

Philosophers who have said that metaphysical arguments issue in verbal recommendations would not give that account of the cow and dog case that would be given by logical positivism. They would not agree that if the dispute does not concern the logical consequences of certain propositions, or the truth of a statement of fact, then the 'dispute' has no sense and no point. Granted, they say, the question is no longer a question of fact, since all the data about the cow and her movements and the dog and his movements are known; and it is not to be met by a logical analysis. The disputants are disputing the choice of a word. In this case either word will do, provided the peculiarities of the situation are understood.

The dispute about the cow and dog seems comparable to a philosophical issue; and to some extent, just as Russell's translation was taken as a model solution by the positivists, puzzle cases of the cow and dog kind provided a model solution for the 'recommendations' theorists. For example. A philosopher who says that physical objects do not exist is not, in an ordinary sense, ignorant of what chairs and tables are. He does not *act* like a man who, as we say, really believes this, but like one who has no doubts whatever, thus provoking Moore's comment that philosophers 'have been able to hold sincerely, as part of their philosophical creed, views inconsistent with what they themselves *knew* to be true'. The verbalist (as we may call the 'recommendations' theory) account of disputes of the cow and dog kind suggests an explanation of Moore's remark. A sceptical philosopher is not disputing any matters of fact for he is just as familiar with the facts as anyone else. He is not, except in a Pickwickian sense, *denying* anything at all; instead he is recommending a way of speaking about the facts and urging the adoption of one, rather than another, verbal notation.

The contrast with positivism is clear in the case of the problem of perception. A form of the verbalist theory dealing with this problem has come to be known as the 'alternative language' thesis. Philosophical theories of perception are not explanations of the facts of perception, they are disguised proposals to use an alternative way of speaking about the things which a person sees. Thus a philosopher who says people never see physical objects, but only sense-data, is not reporting any ordinary or extraordinary facts of experience; he is not, as his words give him the appearance of doing, proposing a new hypothesis which could be empirically verified. Nor is he uttering nonsense. What he is doing 'is simply to recommend a new verbal usage. He is proposing to us that instead of speaking for example, of seeing a straight stick which looks crooked ... we should speak of seeing a sense-datum which really has the quality of being crooked, and which belongs to a straight stick'.[1] In the opening declaration of 'Philosophical Perplexity' Wisdom expounds the same tactics:

> A philosophical answer is really a verbal recommendation in response to a request which is really a request with regard to a sentence which lacks a conventional use whether there occur situations which could conventionally be described by it.

> Thus the sceptic's pretended doubts amount to pointing out that, unlike statements descriptive of sensations, statements about material things make sense with 'perhaps he is mistaken'.

> The sceptic's doubts become then a recommendation to use 'know' only with statements about sense-experience and mathematics and to prefix *all* other statements with 'probably'.[2]

A philosopher is choosing almost arbitrarily between different forms of expression:

> The important point is ... that we have a choice of different notations for describing the same observations, the choice being determined only by the greater convenience of one notation, or our personal inclination, or by tossing a coin.[3]

[1] A. J. Ayer, *The Foundations of Empirical Knowledge*, London 1958, p. 25.

[2] *Philosophy and Psycho-Analysis*, pp. 36, 45. Wisdom would not give the same account of the matter today. See Chapter VIII, Section 3, of the present work.

[3] G. A. Paul, 'Is there a Problem about Sense-Data?', *Logic and Language* (1st series), ed. A. Flew, Oxford 1952, pp. 112–13.

The operative reasons behind these moves are again the same dogmas: the verbalist treatment of sceptical doubts is a variation of the essential structure of Hume's argument. All the circumstances are known to the observers, further empirical investigation has no relevance, therefore the issue cannot concern a matter of fact and does not concern matters of logic; yet rival views are still advanced. What remains, and here is the change from Hume, is a decision about the choice of a word. Professor Lazerowitz, perhaps the most forceful representative of this position, observes that a philosophical sceptic 'when faced with a fact which apparently disestablishes his view' does not accept this as a refutation but 'brings forward an argument'; however a philosopher 'cannot both know the facts and urge that it is nevertheless a correct argument against them'. The fulcrum of his theory is a revised version of the Humean and positivist dichotomy:

> Philosophical views *have no refutations*. If no considerations, either of the sort which disestablish empirical theories or of the sort which disestablish *a priori* ones, are *relevant* to them, then they are neither empirical nor *a priori*. It makes no sense to speak of refuting them, nor, for that matter, of proving them.[1]

It remains for him to make the established move of bringing philosophy within the compartments of the division or rejecting it outright; or to place philosophical pronouncements in a third class of 'arguments' incapable of proving or refuting, and 'conclusions' incapable of being true or false. A sceptic's argument 'is not designed to establish the truth of any view, empirical or *a priori*. It is meant to back a *verbal recommendation*. His "views" are really proposals with regard to the use of ordinary expressions.'[2]

Along with this diagnosis of metaphysics the verbalist theory developed its own thesis about the proper conduct of philosophical investigation. Philosophy is in the first instance a corrective undertaking designed to unravel metaphysical tangles; it is the job of 'philosophy' to do well what 'metaphysics' does badly, to set out clearly and in full the grammatical features which a metaphysician reveals obscurely and inadequately. The logical analysis of statements is abandoned as a dogma of philosophical method and replaced by a new

---

[1] *The Structure of Metaphysics*, London 1955, p. 18.   [2] Ibid., p. 19.

descriptive technique: a metaphysical question is really a request for 'a description of those features of the use of the expressions involved in the questions which incline one to answer "Yes", and of those features of their use which incline one to answer "No"'.[1] A dispute is settled, or rather 'dissolved' by describing in full the aspects of the situation that induce conflicting philosophical views; no more need, or could, be done. Although Hume and positivism condemned metaphysics as spurious the verbalist view is more charitable. Metaphysical statements point to hidden likenesses and differences between different types of statements and reveal verbal peculiarities not exhibited in common usage; they show linguistic penetration. Yet it is a short step from saying that philosophical problems are not solved but dissolved, to saying that they are not problems at all. The point of talking in terms of their 'dissolution' is to stress that they are quite unlike ordinary factual or logical problems, since they originate from misunderstandings and confusions of a special linguistic sort: clear them up and the problems disappear.

The 'recommendations' view is a theory in transition and thus differs from the fixed and pivotal moves of the positivist and Humean accounts. The chief departure is its rejection of the idea that a place for philosophy must be found within the domains of science or logic. Its chief failure is its unsatisfactory and wavering account of the new location. Despite Wisdom's observation that extravagant philosophical theories are more than symptoms of linguistic confusion, what more they are was at the time imperfectly and incompletely grasped. There is a reason for this. The key problem of all three theories, posed in its complexity by Hume and in its simplicity by the cow and dog case, remained unanswered: How can knowledge be gained once there is no question of further investigation or demonstration? The merit and the advance of the 'recommendations' story was to take this problem with a new seriousness.

5. *Philosophy and knowledge*

Bankers and shopkeepers can add, subtract, do long-division and algebra with no knowledge, or even with erroneous knowledge, of the

---

[1] *Philosophy and Psycho-Analysis*, p. 100.

theory of the nature of arithmetic. A misconception, or no conception at all, of the nature of mathematics has no bad or good influence on the ordinary practice of accounting and calculation. In philosophy the position is different. A misapprehension of the nature of the arguments employed will usually, if not always, appear in a mishandling of those same arguments. The connection between theory and practice is more intimate here than elsewhere. One reason why is this. A theory of the nature of mathematics need not itself be a mathematical theory; but a theory of the nature of philosophy is always a philosophical one, thus excellencies and deficiencies in the theoretical half more easily carry over into actual practice. To philosophize about philosophy and to philosophize about ethics or perception, is in both cases to philosophize. It follows from this intimate connection between the philosophical investigation of philosophical reasoning and the philosophical investigation of the reasoning of moralists and mathematicians, scientists and men in the street, that the two levels of investigation must be scrutinized together if either one is to be understood. The character of philosophy can be assessed only by turning to the workings and operations of specific philosophical problems. General speculations about what philosophy should or must be like are not enough; the answers lie in an inspection of the mechanics of particular issues. A number of these issues, therefore, are taken up in the following chapters as documents of both the power and the inadequacy of the dogmas set out here.

Philosophical doubts about knowledge have been, and deserve to be, the centre of attention in any such investigation. It is not an historical accident that accounts of the nature of philosophical reasoning have been given collaterally with attempts to deal with the problems raised by a sceptic, for these problems display what is most characteristic of philosophical inquiry. They force us to face the difficulty of explaining a type of reasoning that results in conclusions which seem both impossible to accept and impossible to neglect. The moves which a sceptic makes in one sector of philosophy are easily transferred to other different sectors; their logic is portable. The reasoning a sceptic employs in the problems of perception (for instance) can be taken up with little alteration in problems to do with the mind or with ethics. This inter-mural dexterity signals the cardinal position of sceptical arguments.

Scepticism about knowledge is also scepticism about philosophical knowledge. Yet there is a difference and a difficulty. Moore could say he knew he had two hands, that he was sitting on a chair, and so on, without reservation or second thoughts. Scepticism about common knowledge is opposed by common sense. But scepticism about philosophical knowledge has no similar and convenient common sense opposition. When the plain man affirms that he *knows* he is sitting on a chair, he is not telling anyone anything new, or reporting something he has just found out for himself. When a philosopher concludes a philosophical point he is attempting to report more than what everyone knows; and one is not, as in the plain man case, always inclined to assent immediately on the basis of what one knows, but perhaps only after some reflection. There is a difference between recognizing the face of an old friend one meets on the street, and learning a new fact about his character from reflecting on one's recollections of his behaviour over a course of years; yet in neither case does one take steps to acquire new data about him. We may wonder how a philosopher can tell anyone anything more than what everyone knows, when everyone knows as much as he does about that which he says he has something new to say. Understanding the character of philosophy is very much a matter of understanding the source of this wondering and the inclinations it creates.

2

Questions of Fact

1. *Foreword*

Some questions of fact are more difficult to answer than others. Sometimes this difficulty is due to a lack of needed observation, in John Wisdom's phrase, to a need for further 'looking and listening'. But sometimes this difficulty is not due to the inadequacy of the data available to those persons attempting an answer, and so not to be met by observing more than they have observed already. On such occasions the use of one's reason and imagination counts more than the use of one's eyes and ears, and the need is for deliberation rather than for investigation, for more thought and discussion rather than for more data. To take a case. It is a matter of fact whether Jones is careless or not. It is also a matter of fact whether Jones did such and such and such and such. Now it may be certain that he did these things and yet be uncertain in the light of them that he is careless; none of the persons attempting an answer may ask for more information about his actions beyond that information already before them, yet they may reach a reasoned decision that he is careless and be right. They may do this without at any point making an inductive or a deductive step. This is commonplace, an ordinary instance of ordinary practice and not an extraordinary or paradoxical feat. Yet it follows from the doctrine under consideration here, that if this case is not impossible it is mysterious, and the mystery of the procedure is as good as an impossibility.

2. *Do all questions of fact call for further observation?*

It is a feature of the traditional theory that inductive reasoning is the proper, indeed the only, procedure appropriate to settling questions of fact. In the widest sense of the word, an inference is inductive when

17

it passes from particular contingent statements recording observed events to a contingent conclusion recording events which they do not entail. Defined in this way induction becomes the sole legitimate method by which fresh statements about matters of fact are ascertained on the grounds of data already at hand, and these statements are subject to confirmation or rejection in the light of subsequent empirical disclosures. Linked with the tendency to regard induction as a model of reasoning about matters of fact is the belief that every question of fact is a request for further empirical investigation and that every answer is, in effect, an empirical hypothesis: involved in the verification of a factual claim is the ever present anticipation of confirmatory data. Accordingly the truth or falsehood of an empirical assertion turns upon the outcome of further inquiries rather than further deliberation.

In its general drift this is a plausible and favourite interpretation of the principle that some observations must be relevant in the verification of a statement of fact if it is to be significant. Yet the principle is ambiguous as it stands, and although it supports this view it can equally support another: for it is unclear whether the principle requires that in order to ascertain the truth-value of an empirical proposition additional empirical observations must always be undertaken, or whether, in some cases, a reasoned conclusion may be drawn directly from the observations already made.

The first interpretation draws support from the argument that in order to ascertain the answer to a question of fact a person must do more than deliberate, reflect or consider the results of empirical investigation done in the past; in so far as there is doubt about the truth of an answer, this doubt arises because the data available are insufficient to determine the answer, and the doubt can be overcome only by making good the deficiency. For if it is not the case that further empirical investigation is needed, and if all the data required to verify an answer are known to those persons attempting to verify that answer, then any further dispute concerning it ceases to be dispute about a question of fact. In short, there is no genuine dispute at all, or alternatively the disputants are not contesting the facts but the choice of a verbal notation. On this view the necessary condition of the lack of a right answer to a question of fact is a failure to fulfil the observations required to confirm it, and to hold otherwise is to admit the possibility that the answer to an empirical question could be determined by reasoning alone, given the basis of observations to date.

If a person knows all the facts at issue, how can he come by deliberation to know anything about them that he does not already know? The question requests a procedure for going beyond the empirical data without taking an observational step, requiring that from a basis of known observations a person reach fresh knowledge about them by a procedure of reasoning alone. Coming close to the rationalist thesis that knowledge of matters of fact can be attained by *a priori* reflection, this request seems suspect; for it appears to undermine the leading empiricist principle that there can be no *a priori* knowledge of the world. The problem to be dealt with can be set by asking whether legitimate disagreement in belief about matters of fact can survive agreement about the material circumstances. We shall see that the answer depends upon the further question of whether there is any form of rational argument that can be employed to bring the dispute to a close. If there is no means of settling the dispute once observational procedures are eliminated, then there are no grounds for supposing the issue to be a genuine conflict, and the way is open to explain the 'disagreement' as more a muddle than a controversy.

3. *Deduction and knowledge of fact*

There is a case for saying that information about matters of fact can be gained by deliberation, if we consider situations in which a contingent conclusion is derived by deduction from contingent premises. It is commonly believed by statisticians, businessmen and military strategists, as well as by others, that the use of deduction is a means whereby one's knowledge of complicated facts can be increased without resorting to experiments and field-surveys, and in this sense new knowledge of fact would appear to be discovered by the agency of a rational process not involving further empirical investigation. Attractive as this belief is, it has been said to be erroneous: for if a person *knows* a contingent proposition then, it will be argued, there is a sense in which he also knows its logical consequences, and by drawing its implications he cannot be said to know what he did not know before making the inference; the conclusion cannot have an empirical content greater than the premises, and to know the premises is *ipso facto* to know the conclusion.

The argument is implausible, but it has a point of some value. Sometimes a person will put forward a proposition he knows is true which he would not have put forward if he had known its logical consequences. This familiar pitfall for debaters and politicians has a logical explanation. From 'X knows P' and 'Q is a logical consequence of P' nothing follows as to whether X does or does not know Q; if P entails Q then a person who asserts P and denies Q contradicts himself, although a person who remarks that he knew P but did not know Q says what might as a matter of fact be true. To suppose that by asserting he knows P a person has thereby asserted Q is simply a slip; for he may have asserted a proposition having an implication of which he was unaware. A man who knows that the matchbox in his pocket is a cube may when asked 'Has it eight or twelve edges?' reply that he is not sure which. He may quickly count the edges to find out. Or he might recollect and reflect that a cube has twice as many edges as sides and that a cube has six sides, so the matchbox has twelve edges. The fact that he proceeds to answer the question in this second way does not show that what he learned by doing this is any less new to him or to the questioner than what he might have learned if he had answered in the first way. Whether deductive inferences do result in new information is a contingent question and the answer, from seeing what happens, is that they do.

Nevertheless it might be thought that the kind of 'knowledge' which a person gains by recognizing the consequences of a contingent proposition which he knows is really psychological, in the sense that it may be new knowledge for him but not for anyone else. If a person had, for instance, the mind of God, he would grasp all the implications in a single sweep, and to go on and express them in terms of analytic propositions would not add to his knowledge. This speculation establishes nothing, even if we leave aside the argument that God is a special case; for the contention comes to saying only that if a person knows all the implications of his assertion then it follows that he knows them. The point of introducing God is just that he is defined as a being that lacks no knowledge, and procedures of deductive inference, or of induction for that matter, have no surprises for him. More serious is the claim that the novelty of the information gained by demonstrative inference is psychological, for it must be admitted that in a sense to be explained this is true. That it could not be otherwise becomes plain when we consider that a person who asserts that p is true contradicts another who asserts that p is false, although a person who asserts of himself that he knows p does not contradict another person who asserts of himself that he does not know p. The difference between the position of these two persons is as contingent as the difference between a person who knows French and a person who does not. And this is what the charge of psychologism is meant to reveal. It is not self-contradictory to claim, with regard to any particular person who has satisfied conditions which entitle us to say he knows p, that he might not have satisfied them and so might not have known p. This 'relativity' of knowledge not only refers to the fact that one person may know propositions which another does not; it also refers to the fact that this inequality may be present even when both persons have an equal knowledge of the data from which the propositions they assert are derived, and it is this feature which encourages the contingent difference between them to be described as a *psychological* difference. Thus the charge of psychological novelty is more easily levelled at knowledge reached by deductive reflection, than in a case where information is obtained by empirical investigation. Yet this is only to point out that the contingent difference between a person who knows p, and a person who does not know p, may be no more than that the one person has successfully carried out thought and deliberation with regard to the data at issue, whereas the other has not. From the fact that knowledge is in this sense psychological it does not follow that it is not knowledge.

This may seem unsatisfactory on other grounds, however. It can be argued that even if a person does not know the implications of his assertion, if he draws them he still does not to add to his knowledge, but merely makes explicit the concealed consequences of what he already knows. As it stands this will not do. Is there any reason why 'making concealed assertions explicit' should not be a way of coming to know some matters of fact? It is precisely by making explicit the consequences of contingent propositions which he knows, that a person can come to know more than he, or perhaps anyone else, knew before. During World War II it was discovered by deduction from reports of observations that the proportions of ships lost through submarine attack was lower in large than in small convoys. It is obviously false to say that nothing, in this case, was gained by deduction. What the sceptical denial does is to call attention to the *difference* between obtaining information about matters of fact by procedures of further observation, and obtaining factual information by deduction from statements descriptive of data already observed. But this difference in the method of investigation does not mean that there must be difference in the knowledge of the results. A sceptic has disclosed that a question of fact can go unanswered for the lack of reasoning rather than the lack of data.

One source of scepticism of this kind lies in the conflation of tautologies and trivial propositions. In the case discussed the formulation of the argument, passing by deduction from contingent premises to contingent conclusions, is tautologous; accordingly, it is tempting to suppose that the inference, being no more than the assertion of a tautology, and expressing in its conclusion nothing not implied by the premises, could result in no more than trivial information given a knowledge of the premises. But the fallacy here is plain. It is an *a priori* matter whether a proposition is a tautology, and a contingent matter whether a proposition is trivial; thus to suppose that because a proposition is a tautology it is therefore trivial is a complete mistake. To say that a tautology is trivial emphasizes that it makes no difference which of the equivalent words or expressions one uses, that the difference is itself trivial. Of course, it may make no difference; but this depends on the character of the occasion and not on the tautologous form of the proposition. What is it about a proposition that makes it 'uninformative' or 'trivial'? The answer depends on something quite apart from its logical form, and is not to be given *a priori*. If some tautologies are monumentally boring, others are especially informative. Suppose that a person is told that it is forty-five kilometres to Paris and asks, 'What is that in miles?' Even though (as we say) there is no difference between 'forty-five kilometres' and 'twenty-eight miles', to the person who asks the question the difference may be that between an accurate or an inaccurate appreciation of the distance, between getting there on time or running out of petrol, between catching or missing a plane. By uttering the words 'forty-five kilometres is twenty-eight miles' one may alter not only a particular way of speaking but also the understanding and grasp of a situation which a particular way of speaking conveys. A question requesting a transformation of words in accord with the strictest rules can be a request for a better apprehension of the facts.

This throws light on a cluster of puzzles subsumed under the name of 'the paradox of analysis'. A representative version goes in this way: If the *analysandum* and the *analysans* are one and the same proposition, only a tautology is produced and nothing is gained; if they are different propositions something is gained, but the *analysans* is no longer an analysis of the *analysandum*. In short: if P and Q are equivalent then they are identical, but if identical how can the one express anything the other does not? The paradox is not, to begin with, a logical paradox; but arises from not noticing that it often does make a difference which words are used when the words at issue are logically equivalent. The very generality of the question makes it perplexing at the start. One is naturally puzzled about how the logical symmetry of equivalent expressions can be reconciled with the contingent asymmetry of the information they convey.

Notice that a person may be puzzled about how a change simply in the form of expression can be informative in a case where *no* logical equivalence is asserted, and that when we come down to instances this is less puzzling than it seems. A man facing a difficult decision may make the state of his emotions more clear to others by saying 'its's like civil war' than by giving a literal description. The expressions 'A lion' and 'The king of the beasts' do not name two different creatures yet the difference between the expressions is not negligible. Often when a listener does not understand what is said to him a speaker will reply 'Let me put this in another way' or 'In other words . . .' even though he repeats the same point. Of course these illustrations are removed from tautologies. Yet they hint at the fallacy of the belief that if two expressions are logically equivalent we are not better off with one than with the other. The difference *may* be trivial, e.g. to substitute 'male parent' for 'father' leaves things right where they were. And by fastening on models like this, designed specifically to underline the equivalence of the expressions, the charge of triviality is generalized to cover all examples. But not all examples are like this model, as the expression 'forty-five kilometres is twenty-eight miles' shows. A difference in the *presentation* of the facts can mean a difference in a *grasp* of the facts.

The paradox is created partly by its formulation. One should ask, instead: In a case where P and Q are equivalent, does the one expression describe the situation to which both refer in a way that is more intelligible, striking, recognizable, familiar and clear than the other? This no longer over-emphasizes the importance of the logical equivalence at the expense of neglecting that re-phrasing the expression of a proposition can result in an increased grasp of the case it describes. The logical truth that P and Q are equivalent is compatible with the contingent fact that Q is more readily understood than P. An analysis can be both demonstrative and informative without any inconsistency or paradox. The apparent dilemma results from the false supposition that there is an incompatibility between the assertion of a logical equivalence and the assertion of an informative proposition.

If we ask why philosophers have supposed this to be true, the reason is not to be found only in the belief that demonstrative reasoning can yield no empirical surprises, but in the wider assumption that fresh knowledge of fact results only from the discovery of new data: that to add to knowledge is necessarily to increase the number of observations. The difference between these is more than negligible, for the latter assumption excludes not only procedures of deductive reasoning. It excludes *any* attempt to justify empirical statements without further empirical investigation.

4. *Questions to be answered by thinking without deducing*

We must ask whether in a situation in which all the empirical data are known, a question of fact could ever be answered by reasoning that does *not* involve a deductive inference. A likely objection is that the word 'reasoning' has no application outside the boundaries of the two favoured methods of argument, and the answer must be 'No'. This objection will be seen to be false as we go along and some piecemeal problems need to be taken up first. The present problem is to decide whether a question of fact can be answered correctly by non-deductive deliberation from the data as they stand. The most conclusive way to decide is to describe a case illustrating that this is possible, for at issue is the contention that no such case can be given.

There is no difficulty in finding cases that will do; or rather, the difficulty is one of appreciating situations whose familiarity hinders recognition. For example, a person who looks at a patch of cloth and when asked 'What colour is it?' hesitates, and then looks at a colour sample and says 'This is yellow' and then says 'The cloth is yellow', is not proceeding, or reasoning, inductively or deductively. Nor is a person who *a.* when asked 'How many edges has this?' looks at a matchbox and says 'This has twelve edges', or *b.* when asked the same question looks at a cube and says 'This has twelve edges' and then says 'This matchbox has twelve edges'. Again, if a person who is asked 'Are there enough cups on this tray and saucers on that tray so that six people can each have a cup and saucer?' looks at the cups and then at the saucers and says 'Yes', his procedure may involve no more than looking and thinking. In these cases certain conditions must be fulfilled: the question must be a question of fact, as must be the answer to it; the procedure employed to answer it must not involve anything more than a study of the data with regard to which the question is asked; and this procedure must not be a logical demonstration.

Of course, these conditions would not have been fulfilled if these questions could not have been answered for the reason that some relevant data were missing at the time. In a shop a person finds what appears to be a map of the United States; it appears to be such for it is folded up and only a small part is visible showing a recognizable bit of coastline. In this case, to answer a question about what it is, by saying that it is a map of the United States, is to predict that when unfolded a number of specific features will be disclosed, the coastline of California, the boundaries with Mexico and Canada, and so on; thus the inference proceeds from observations now in hand to the results of observations yet to be made. But the questions in the previous examples are not of this kind. Unlike the present case, nothing in the way of relevant data is concealed. Both the Questioner and the Answerer have before them the data they need; they are in the position, for instance, of persons who are studying a completely unfolded map and attempting to determine what it is. The peculiarity of the cases under consideration is that the

c

questions call for reasoned decisions when the difficulty of deciding is *not* due to a lack of data.

This feature, especially, is likely to be brought forward as evidence that the initial conditions have not been fulfilled: for it might be supposed that under such circumstances no answer given could describe any matter of fact, or that the question itself is not a contingent question. And the reason given is this: a statement is the type of statement which it is, because it has a verificational procedure appropriate to that type; thus a statement is contingent if it has the method of verification of a contingent statement and, this objection states, with the possible exception of statements a person makes about his sensations, this method *necessarily* involves further empirical investigation; since the statements in the examples do not have *this* verificational characteristic they are not contingent: they do not assert any matters of fact. Yet it is clear that a person who looks at a cloth and says 'This is yellow' or a person who says 'This matchbox has twelve edges', or 'There are enough cups and saucers here for six people' *is* making a contingent statement describing the circumstances and asserting some matter of fact. Underlying this objection is the supposition that factual verification must proceed in accord with a *single* model, e.g. the example of the folded map.

A feature that might be taken to cast doubt here is that these answers, especially the answer 'This is yellow', are *obvious*. As obvious, for example, as the answer to the question of how many letters there are in the word 'cat'. However, the obviousness or unobviousness of the answer has no bearing on the matter of the statement's logical position; for even if it should happen that everyone who was asked a certain question was always able to answer correctly, straight away, this alone would not show that it was, or was not, a question of fact. There is a difference in degree between an occasion on which a person looks at an object in question and replies immediately, and an occasion on which a person who looks at an object, hesitates, and does not reply until after he has thought about it. Examples of questions that are easy to answer move by degrees into examples where the answer calls for substantial reflection. For if a feature of an obvious case of kind K is altered, this change may leave it such that the answer to the question whether it is of kind K is now more obscure, although the question itself is neither more nor less obscure than before; it remains the same, and so the logical position of the answer to it in a difficult case is not different in kind from the logical position of the answer to it in an easy case. The difference is that a procedure of deliberation now plays a larger part in reaching a decision than before.

For illustration take a more complex case in which deliberation determines the result. It is an action in the law courts. The plaintiff was a Russian princess whose husband had been mainly responsible for the killing of Rasputin. The defendant produced a film on the life of Rasputin in which a Russian princess was portrayed as having been seduced by him. In the course of the action the jury were made thoroughly acquainted with all the facts at issue and instructed to determine whether a seduction had been portrayed. They found it had. But the conclusion was not reached by deduction from the information they had been considering. As in all such cases both questions of fact and questions of law are involved: it is a question of fact for the jury to decide whether the film showed the plaintiff as having been seduced; it is a question of law for the judge whether the portrayal of a seduction is defamatory within the meaning of the law. The jury were not attempting to answer a question in a situation in which some material facts were missing, such that they would be instructed to reach a decision on the balance of probabilities; as, for example, in a case where the evidence suggests that a person stole a certain item although no one saw him do it. In the action for defamation no relevant data were missing and there was no question that more evidence could have any bearing on the matter. The point is that even if the jury have all the data before them a question of fact still remains to be answered, and the procedure for reaching a verdict about what happened is one of non-deductive deliberation. Of course, in a case like this there will be reason on both sides and perhaps more on one side than on the other. So we must reckon with the fact that disagreement about the description of the circumstances can continue despite the irrelevance of additional data. This is not disagreement in belief about the outcome of rival predictions, but disagreement to be resolved by the outcome of argument involving no predictions at all: a matter of appreciating what is there to be seen by anyone, and not of anticipating what no one could have seen at the time.

There are occasions on which the answer to a question of fact does not meet the puzzlement which prompts the question itself. A man can answer a question by describing the situation to which the question refers in meticulous, photographic detail, and this answer can be correct. He may correctly answer the question whether a person's action was careless by saying 'Well, he made a right-hand turn and did not signal or look to see what was behind him'. Yet this answer may not meet the demands of the question, since the questioner may lack no knowledge of the circumstances described in the answer; it may still not be clear to him whether the action was careless. He requires an answer that goes beyond the narrative he knows, one which compares the present circumstances with other comparable circumstances, or we could say *places* the case at issue with respect to cases of carelessness which he understands.

5. *Borderline cases*

Although reflective issues before the courts are among the borderline puzzles that best exhibit the characteristics of deliberative reasoning they are not the only, or the most common, examples. If someone removes the wheels from a caravan and puts it up on blocks in his garden there is an element of difficulty in clearly distinguishing the caravan from a shed or summer house that was not present before the alteration. It can be puzzling whether a certain object is a cup, a beaker or a mug. The parents of a child can disagree whether he resembles his father more than his mother though they lack no knowledge of the child's appearance, characteristics, traits and habits. It may not be an issue whether a cottage is missing a few slates and in need of paint, yet disputed whether it is dilapidated. In these cases different though incompatible accounts of the same situation can be plausibly advanced.

There is a tendency to suppose that borderline disputes are, or are in the end, disagreements about the usage of words. The thesis is attractive: if two persons agree about all of the observed facts, then any continuing disagreement in the absence of the need for additional observations is a sign that the dispute has now entered a verbal phase; the one party to the dispute is not denying any matter of fact (beyond a matter of verbal usage) asserted by the other, and if either of them is making a mistake the only possible mistake there is now room to make is a mistake about the ordinary word to use.

Disagreements having a factual air may, certainly, be disguised verbal issues. When two people have their eyes on the same object and one of them says 'The tea caddy is on the tray' while the other objects 'No, it's the tea cosy', one or the other may be confused about the correct word for the thing. The dispute is easy to settle with the aid of a dictionary or a knowledgeable friend. There are more complicated cases having the same basic solution. The English usage of the expression 'first floor' is equivalent to the American usage of the expression 'second floor'. Understandably an Englishman and an American who do not know this might take issue about which floor of a building they are on; and they may believe they are contesting a statement of fact until they are told, or work out for themselves, the missing linguistic equation. These examples exhibit a confusion similar to that of the visitor to the zoo who calls a llama an alpaca, and an alpaca a llama. Just as the remedy for him is to look at the guide book or summon a keeper, the answer in general is found by attending to the regulations and practice of common and correct usage.

Partly because of their common occurrence and partly also because of their simple solutions, incidents like these tend to occupy a more central place than they deserve in our thinking about disagreements which survive the need for observations. Like conceptual magnets they pull superficially similar cases into their own special orbits. Accordingly it must be made clear at the start that borderline disputes have little relation to verbal dislocations like the ones above.

The main point of difference is that in a genuinely borderline situation a question of fact can remain unanswered even if all the facts about ordinary usage are known. Disagreement about a borderline case can arise when there is no disagreement about the ordinary meanings of the words involved; indeed it is a requirement of a genuine borderline case that the ordinary meanings be understood. Take the instance of the Englishman and the American and suppose, this time, that the building in which they are standing is placed on the side of a hill so that the floors are confusingly arranged with respect to the ground. They are now clear about each other's conventional usage but still disagree: one claims that they are standing on the first floor and the other denies it. In this case what creates the problem is a peculiarity in the *situation* and not a mistake about ordinary usage. Again, suppose two men are seated at a chessboard moving the chessmen in a typically skilful way, but each is listening to a telephone giving the moves of a game going on elsewhere and placing the pieces accordingly. A difference of opinion about whether they are playing chess is not a sign that the ordinary usage of the words 'playing chess' is being misunderstood. For the case itself is unusual, idiosyncratic.

The comparison can be made with a different example. Two people unsure of the language may discuss whether the English word 'wood' is used only as the name of the material that comes from trees, or also as the name of a place where trees are found. Here, they are ignorant of some facts of ordinary language and an investigation of standard usage is appropriate. On the other hand, two people who know the language may discuss whether the word 'wood' applies to a specific group of trees they both know. This problem is altogether different for they are trying to understand the degree of likeness between the group of trees in point and typical occasions on which the word is correctly applied. There is no question of the problem being settled by appealing to what one would ordinarily say; even to those who know what would be said in an ordinary case, it may not be clear what should be said in this case.

In these examples the question is not 'What are the ordinary words to use in this case?' but rather, 'Do the words that ordinarily apply to ordinary cases also apply here?'. This is not something that can be found out by consulting dictionaries or paying heed to users of standard language. A definition may provoke only the further question of whether the definition is, or is not, applicable to the case. A dictionary which defines 'first floor' as 'the floor above the ground floor' is no aid to deciding whether the present floor is the first floor or the floor above the ground floor. Its job is to explain and expand the use of the word on typical and uncontested occasions; it is a guide to explored, not unexplored, cases. Nor is a solution to be found by appealing to the ordinary usage of the words. Information from this quarter is superfluous, since a borderline dispute could not arise unless the disputants already understand what the words at issue ordinarily mean. A person must have the capacity to recognize and to use words correctly on typical occasions before recognizing and judging off-centre instances. One may hesitate over an answer in the borderline examples above precisely because there are some clear occasions of 'being on the first floor', 'being a wood' and 'playing chess' where one would not hesitate. The explicit recognition of a borderline case is an implicit acknowledgement that typical situations are understood; and the existence of a borderline puzzle is a proof that there are, by comparison, typical cases where there is no puzzle. The job is to close or sustain the gap between them.

It will help a person faced with a borderline case to indicate affinities and differences between the situation that puzzles him and other situations that do not; to compare standard cases where he knows a word applies with intermediate cases, and so work towards the case at issue. This is a matter of judgement and the appreciation of the fine points of a resemblance.

Examples of borderline situations illustrate that contestable matters of fact are not always hypotheses testable by future experience. But not all problems of fact calling for reflection are borderline. Two persons may scan carefully the same page and only one of them may recognize the misprints on it; even though there may be nothing borderline about it, the difference between them is still not that one of them has observed more, but that one is more observant. And being in this way observant is often the difference between success and failure. For example, let us suppose that four people are seated round a table playing cards. The game is draw poker. The first player takes up his cards one by one. After picking up a ten of clubs he could predict with complete assurance that he will not pick up another ten of clubs; he could predict with near certainty that he will not go on to pick up a jack of clubs, a queen of clubs, a king of clubs and an ace of clubs; and if he had picked up a ten, jack, queen and king of clubs, he could predict, though with much less certainty, that he will not pick up a further club. But predicting cards yet to come from cards that have come so far is not the whole of poker. Once a player has before him all the cards he is going to get he must still decide from those cards what it is that he has in his hand, and a skilful player may apprehend immediately what a poor player never notices, or notices only after some thought. Suppose at the end of a hand a player lays his cards on the table where they can be seen and says to the others that he has three jacks. They nod assent; but the man on his right is concerned. 'Look', he says, 'the fact is you have more than that. You know the deuces are wild. Well you have a jack of hearts, two deuces, a ten of clubs and an eight of hearts, that is, three jacks *or* a jack-high straight.' His words describe no cards beyond those that all the players see and yet to the player who put down the hand they describe something that he and the others did not see. This situation is only too familiar to card players. When removed from the laboratory conditions of the card table to the diffuse and tangled conditions of real life this kind of situation is only infrequently isolated in its pure state. Rather, like an entire evening at cards, it consists in a mixture of reflective and predictive activities with the combination sometimes orderly and sometimes kaleidoscopic. Like the card game also, success in both is requisite for winning the big stakes. Neither the player who has a poor understanding of his own hands but is superb at predicting the cards to come, nor the player who is hopeless at predicting but brilliant in recognizing what he has, is likely to last the evening without a deficit.

A capacity to carry out comparisons can be the difference between fact-finding and fact-missing in situations where one considers reflectively incidents that have actually happened. A person can have complete before him all the data he needs to answer a question of fact, and in spite of this neither he nor anyone else may see a way to an answer. He can be in the position of someone who does not understand what is happening before his own eyes even though he has seen what is happening and all that is happening again and again. We imagine him seeing the hands of clocks move round, hearing the chimes of clocks and seeing shadows move on sundials; and that he sees the sun rise and set, the movement of the stars and sees these things a hundred times over without realizing what the clocks, chimes or sundials are doing, and without realizing their connections with the sun and stars or night and day. He is like a person who, we imagine, is familiar with thermometers and can describe their performances in minute detail, and is familiar with the weather being cold, hot or temperate, and can describe that in minute detail. But when asked whether there is any connection between the behaviour of thermometers and the weather says, 'So far as I can see there is no connection'. In so far as a person in this position has not seen the hands of the clocks move, not heard the chimes, not watched the sundial, and not observed the sun and stars, or not seen the thermometer rise and fall and not observed that it is cold, hot or temperate, then it is a lack of observation that keeps him in ignorance. But when all these phenomena which he needs to observe have been observed by him, then the information he lacks is no longer due to inadequate observation but to insufficient thought and reflection.

3

Questions of Concepts

1. *Foreword*

Questions of fact can merge into questions of concepts, for what begins as a question of what *is* so can end as a question of what possibly *could* be so. Often, observation and reflection work together to gain an answer. Sometimes, however, observation is neither sufficient nor relevant in answering a question, and sometimes, too, the question may not be one of formal logic or mathematics. When Plato asked what justice is, he was asking a question of this kind. When lawyers ask what negligence is, or when philosophers ask what knowledge is, or how knowledge differs from belief, they also are asking questions of the same kind, questions about concepts. To call them 'questions of concepts' brings out their likeness to *a priori* questions like 'How many edges has a cube?' and their differences from questions that are not *a priori* like 'Is the matchbox in my pocket a cube?' They are questions requesting a grasp of the *connections*, as we say, between a concept and its characteristics. One example would be a question about the logical connections between 'a cube' and 'twelve edges'.

Yet this example is not representative. The philosophically puzzling cases – the cases of justice, knowledge and negligence, for instance – are again different. In these cases the connections that puzzle us between a concept and its characteristics are neither contingent nor necessary, and so are unlike the connection between 'a cube' and 'twelve edges'. For example, 'she is smiling' is a reason in favour of 'she is pleased' though the connection is not contingent, for anyone on learning that she is smiling has, if he understands, some reason for saying she is pleased, although he may be wrong; and, therefore, the connection is not necessary. The idea of non-necessary *a priori* connections seems odd, and no doubt this is due to the hold of the tradi-

34

tional theory as much as anything else. Its consequences are of wide scope and have a direct effect on the philosophical problems of scepticism in epistemology, in ethics, and scepticism about philosophical reasoning itself.

2. How possibilities can have a bearing on what actually happens

We should be impressed that the statement 'B was negligent in sleeping on duty' and the statement 'Sleeping on duty is an example of negligence' though similar are not the same. The verification of the second statement is *a priori*. The first statement asserts a matter of fact; it tells us that a particular person was negligent, that he *did* sleep on duty, and to ascertain this some empirical investigation is called for. Analogously, the basis for answering the question 'Can this child tell the time?' is what a particular child says and does on a number of occasions when asked the time, and like 'Can the child read?' or 'Can the child run?' the question of whether he can tell the time is contingent. Yet it can be debated *a priori* whether the child's performance constitutes, or is a case of, 'telling the time', and whether the answer 'Yes' is justified or not. In which case the non-contingent question 'Is this performance a case of time-telling?' is the one at issue. One might wish to say, obviously the answer to the non-contingent question can have some bearing on the answer to the contingent question. But how is this possible? For it seems that an answer to the one provides no answer to the other. Yet it also seems absurd to deny that persons may reflect on the child's position without making empirical observations and without knowing whether the situation is an actual one, a matter of fact, and ascertain that this constitutes an example, or an illustration, or a case, of time-telling, and that this reflection is somehow relevant to saying what in fact the child is able to do. One seems to be reasoning *a priori* to an *a posteriori* conclusion. Again, one may seem to be reasoning *a posteriori* to an *a priori* conclusion: for by answering the contingent question 'Was B negligent in sleeping on duty?' a person seems also to have answered the question 'Is sleeping on duty a case of negligence?', which could have been answered without empirical investigation, simply by considering conceivable situations.

What begins as a question of fact can launch a conceptual investigation. Perhaps the simplest example is the ancient question whether a particular man is bald, when the amount of hair on his head is such that the question could be raised. The discussion may shift, and probably would, from the question of whether there does exist a particular man (let us call him Smith) alleged to be bald, to the question of whether a person in Smith's position could conceivably be bald: whether, for instance, this is a possible instance of baldness. One might have debated and decided the issue with regard to the possible case independently of the different issue of whether, in fact, any particular person is or is not bald. Let us look again at the case of negligence.

Suppose it is asked, 'Was B negligent in going to sleep on duty?'. It might be replied, 'But B did not go to sleep on duty so he is not negligent'. Both the question and the reply are contingent. Suppose now it is said 'Even though B did not sleep on duty, if he had done so he would have been negligent'; or 'Sleeping on duty is an example of negligence, regardless of whether B, or anyone else, has ever done it; regardless of whether anyone was ever in fact negligent for this reason'. If it is disputed whether sleeping on duty is an example or an instance of negligence, notice that the disputants need not know whether a case of this kind has ever actually occurred: they need not know whether the situation they discuss describes an actual event or merely a possible one and they may treat the situation as purely hypothetical or fictional. In these circumstances reasons can be given for and against saying that the imagined situation is a case of negligence: it is possible to debate and definitely decide the case without making an existential claim. But unlike a debate concerning the statement of fact that B was negligent in sleeping on duty, it is irrelevant in debating the statement 'Sleeping on duty is an example of negligence' to point out that the case concerned never occurred, that it is imaginary and merely possible; this has no bearing on whether the imaginary situation is one of negligence or not. And even if in debating this possible case the disputants do refer, in addition, to actual situations, these situations need not, logically, carry more weight than reference the disputants make to any possible or imaginary situations, for they are not debating whether the case at issue ever in fact occurred: they are attempting to determine whether, if it ever should occur, it would be a case of negligence.

Yet even if it is plain that the question 'Was B negligent in sleeping on duty?' concerns some actual matters of fact and that the answer 'Yes' would have been false if B had not been observed to have slept on duty, it appears that by answering 'Yes' a person is also answering a different though similar question which is not a question of fact, namely 'Is sleeping on duty an instance of negligence?' to which the answer 'Yes' might be true even if no one had done this; even if 'Yes' is a false answer to the question 'Was B negligent in sleeping on duty?' But this seems mistaken for it suggests that a proposition about actual matters of fact, 'B was negligent for he slept on duty', entails a proposition which makes no claim about actual matters of fact, 'Sleeping on duty is an example of negligence'.

Let us look at the case more closely. It is asserted a. that a particular person B is negligent for he did a certain thing, he slept on duty; this assertion entails the proposition b. 'A person who does a certain thing, namely sleeping on duty, is negligent'. Now even if a is as a matter of fact false and describes no existing state of affairs, b may still be true. That is, b can be said to be true (or false) even if there never was or will be a person of whom it is true to say 'That is the person to whom the proposition expressed by b refers'. In order to determine whether b is true it is not necessary to ascertain the truth-value of any contingent proposition. The determination of b is a wholly reflective matter. Although from the contingent assertion a the a priori proposition b may be inferred, notice that this inference has a special characteristic: for it makes no difference to the inference whether a is as a matter of fact true or false, or describes or misdescribes an actual situation. The actuality of the situation to which a refers is beside the point: that a represents an existing or a possible case has no bearing on whether b follows from a; no more than whether the assertion 'There are in this box four fresh eggs and two bad eggs' describes an existing state of affairs has a bearing on whether 'There are in this box at least six eggs' can be inferred. The peculiarity of the inference is that the contingent truth of 'B was negligent in sleeping on duty' is an inessential feature of it and that, though it happens to be an actual case, it is required by the inference only to be a possible case. By taking over the role of a possible case, or an imaginary case, the statement of an actual case can entail an a priori statement.[1]

[1] See Peter Long, 'Possibility and Actuality', *Mind*, April 1961.

But if a contingent statement can entail an *a priori* statement, under these special circumstances, can a contingent statement be entailed by an *a priori* statement? Obviously the statement 'Sleeping on duty is a case of negligence' does not entail any statement to the effect that it actually happened that a person slept on duty and was negligent. This is a matter for empirical investigation. It is possible to decide *a priori* whether a certain *situation* is an example of negligence, but not that such a situation actually existed or does now exist; from a possible situation an existential claim cannot be inferred.

That this is so might be thought, wrongly, to lend support to the belief that a purely deliberative judgement has no relevance in deciding the truth or falsehood of a claim about matters of fact. Suppose it is ascertained by investigation that a situation in which a person went to sleep when it was his duty to stay awake did in fact occur, and that it is now asked in the courts whether this person is negligent. The jury are presented with the details and must decide on a matter of fact, whether *this* person *was* negligent or not. Now even though they are attempting to answer a question of fact it is possible that the reasons which they give for their verdict as to the contingent case might have been given by a person attempting to decide a purely hypothetical, imaginary case. For example, a barrister in his study may have before him the same data which the jury have before them, but, let us suppose, the barrister does not know whether these data describe some actual state of affairs or whether they are simply descriptive of a hypothetical situation. On the basis of these data he may be able to conclude that this is a case of negligence; but he cannot conclude, as the jury can, that a specific person was in fact negligent. By reasoning *a priori* it is possible for him to have carried out the reasoning which would have answered a contingent question, the one before the jury. Or it is possible, for example, for him to have written down his arguments on a sheet of paper and, unknown to him, for someone to have taken this paper and shown it to the jury, and for the jury to have reached a verdict on the basis of these arguments together with the knowledge that the circumstances did actually occur.

To take another instance. Suppose an observer X sees an animal in a field but is unable to say what it is; and that a non-observer Y is given a description of the animal and is able to say what it is but is not told that it describes the animal X has seen. X has observed that there is an animal in the field but does not recognize the kind of animal it is. Y has recognized the kind of animal but has not observed that there is any animal in the field. Between the two of them they have done enough to answer the question of whether there *is* an animal of a certain kind in the field.

By saying that a question of fact can launch a 'double investigation' we mark the feature that an inquiry undertaken in reaching an answer can include both an observational and a reflective phase. When the question at issue concerns events that took place on an actual occasion, deliberation about possible events can be an attempt to understand what the situation actually was on that occasion.

3. *Conceptual connections*

A question can also be puzzling even if the results of observation are given no special regard, leaving it no longer, if it ever was, a question of fact. When it is an indifferent matter whether the events discussed took place, and an irrelevant point whether the case in question is an actual or merely possible or imaginary one, a deliberative procedure can still be an attempt to understand what needs to be understood. A purely reflective review of possible or hypothetical situations can be undertaken with the intention of apprehending the scope, varieties and characteristics of a concept and its relations to other concepts.

In the past philosophers have asked questions like 'What is knowledge?' or 'What is belief?', and these appear to be questions of fact to be settled by empirical investigation. Noticing, however, that investigation of this kind does not yield the answers wanted, the questions have been asked in a new form, e.g. 'What does "knowledge" mean?', 'What is the meaning of "belief"?' which brings out their difference from empirical questions. But this form of question, too, is unsatisfactory for it leads to a demand for an answer to the question 'And what is "meaning"?' The clarity gained by the new form of question in distinguishing it from a plain question of fact is diminished by the obscurity of the answer to the question about meaning. To avoid this, philosophers have asked questions like 'How is the word "knowledge" used?' and 'What is the correct usage of the word "belief"?' This change makes it clear what the question is asking, for it is literally requesting an account of our ordinary practice with words. Yet there is a price to pay: although clarity is again gained, the questions now seem no different in kind from the original question 'What is knowledge?', understood as a question of empirical fact. In order to make plain that the procedure for answering these questions is different from the procedure for answering 'What is' questions like 'What is the population of London?' philosophers have asked, 'What are the necessary and sufficient conditions of knowledge?' or 'What criteria entail a case of belief?' These suggest that *a priori* conceptual questions function only to disclose relations of necessity between a concept C and the feature $f_1 \ldots f_n$ which define it; and that if the question is not to be understood as an *a posteriori* one it must be understood as a demand for an analytic definition. Such questions rightly review possibilities of connection between a concept and its characteristics. But they wrongly look for a *necessary* connection as the only one that will do. Everyone knows the rationalist myth of the necessity of *a posteriori* connections. Less well-known is the empiricist myth of the necessity of *a priori* connections.

That there are non-necessary *a priori* connections between one statement and another, or between reasons and conclusions, can be shown decisively by a number of examples and we should go to them directly at the start. Examples of *a priori* connections which *are* logically necessary are excessively familiar, and it is one of Wittgenstein's points that because of their very familiarity we tend to suppose that *all* cases of connections between reasons and conclusions must conform to this pattern. In the *Investigations* Wittgenstein advises us to *look* at the full range of cases. His advice is well-taken, and to break the hold of the traditional picture we must turn to fresh instances.

a. Imagine that we are playing a guessing game, in which I call out a characteristic feature of a creature and you try to answer by saying what the creature is. I say 'It has feet'; well, this eliminates fish and you say 'A duck'. I say 'Hands and feet' and you think, 'It must be human, a monkey or a gorilla' and say it is a monkey. I say 'It has hands and feet and walks upright' and you reply 'A human being'. In this game I call out characteristics which are reasons counting in favour of the conclusion you reach: that something has feet is a reason to say it is a man or a monkey but not a fish, although insufficient reason to say which. These characteristics are not causally connected with the answers given, rather the connection is *a priori*; to say that a human being has hands and feet and walks upright is to explain in some degree what a human being is, to say in part what 'human being' means. Especially, it is not to say that the characteristic of having hands and feet and walking upright is associated with the predicate 'human being' in virtue of such a fact as that hands and feet have been found in experience almost always associated with those characteristics to which the words 'human being' apply, but rather that hands and feet number among those characteristics: just as having two eyes, or a nose, number among the characteristics referred to by the word 'face', and are not merely causally associated with the variety of criteria for something's being a face. The connection between having hands and feet and being human (or between 'having eyes' or 'having a nose' and 'being a face') resembles the connection between 'having a St George's cross' and 'being a Union Jack' in that these characteristics provide, independently of any contingent association, a reason for asserting that an instance possessing them is one of a certain kind. Yet there is a central difference between the two cases. The statement 'This flag is a Union Jack' entails 'This flag contains a St George's cross', and while 'This flag contains a St George's cross' does not entail 'This flag is a Union Jack', it does so in conjunction with 'This flag contains a St Andrew's and a St Patrick's cross' together with a statement of the appropriate colours and arrangements. But the statement 'This creature is human' does not entail 'This creature has hands and feet' any more than 'This is a face' entails 'This has two eyes'. Thus, in the case of the Union Jack, the omission of a cross of St George or a cross of St Andrew in an instance would be fatal to the correct application of the predicate 'a Union Jack', whereas the omission of hands or of feet, or a nose or an eye, or a chin, would not be fatal to the application of the predicate 'a human being' or 'a face'. Nor does the statement 'This has two eyes' or 'This has a mouth' entail 'This is a face'; nor again does 'This has two hands and two feet' entail 'This is a human being'.

The relationship here between the separate characteristics and the concept is neither causal nor logically necessary; yet it is *a priori*. For the statement 'This creature has hands and feet' is *a reason in favour* of saying 'This creature is human' without necessitating it; and the statement 'This has two eyes' *counts in favour of*, but does not necessitate, 'This is a face'. From the truth of 'X has two arms and two legs' it does not follow that X is human. Obviously, it is not self-contradictory to say 'X has two arms and two legs, although X is not human'. But from the truth of 'X has two arms and two legs' it *does* follow that there is *some reason* which counts in favour of saying that X is human. A person is not entitled to conclude straight away that X *is* human, if all he knows is that X has two arms and two legs; but if he knows what 'human being' means, and knows that X has two arms and two legs, he can conclude that there are *grounds* for supposing that X is human.

b. The statement 'Black is speaking French' is a reason for saying 'Black speaks French' and they stand in relation to each other as 'Black is wearing a hat' stands in relation to 'Black wears a hat', or as 'Black is reading the cricket scores' to 'Black is a cricket follower'. The first of each pair of statements, if true, counts in favour of the truth of the second and does this in a special way: for the truth of the first statement in each case supports the truth of the second, not because it is inductively correlated with the truth of the second, but rather because it describes part of the criteria for saying the second is true; or, it could be said, describe a characteristic which would count in favour of asserting the second statement independently of any contingent facts. Thus the connections between these pairs of statements are unlike causal or contingent connections. They are unlike, for example, the following case: where 'Black is wearing a hat' is a reason for saying 'Black is wearing a bowler' in virtue of a contingent connection arising from observations of his habit of dress; that Black wears a hat does not mean, even in part, that it is often true to say that Black is wearing a bowler. Yet if they are not causal, these connections also have the feature that none of them is logically necessary. It is an *a priori* assertion that 'Black is reading the cricket scores' is a reason in support of saying 'Black is a cricket follower', because being a cricket follower *means* among other things, although does not entail, reading the cricket scores. One could say in advance of any observations that 'Black is reading the cricket scores' is a reason, though not a sufficient reason, to assert that Black is a cricket follower. It would be paradoxical to assert that Black is reading the cricket scores and go on to deny that there is any reason to say he is a cricket follower; it would not be paradoxical to deny he is a cricket follower. And the same can be said of the other cases. That Black speaks French means, among other things, that on some occasions it is true to say that Black is speaking French, but does not entail 'Black is speaking French'. And although 'Black is speaking French' is, independently of any matter of fact, a reason in favour of saying that Black speaks French, it does not entail 'Black speaks French': the former may be true and the latter false, for it may be that Black is uttering at the moment the only French sentence he knows; yet someone on being told that Black is speaking French at the moment has been given a reason to think that Black speaks French. Or again, that Black wears a hat means, in part, that it is often true to say he is wearing a hat, but does not entail 'Black is wearing a hat'; nor does 'Black is wearing a hat' entail that Black wears a hat, he might be wearing it for a joke. In each case the connection between the pairs of statements is logical yet not logically necessary.

It comes out of examples *a* and *b* that on some occasions the presence in an instance I of a certain characteristic C can count in favour of saying that I is an instance of predicate P in virtue of C being part of what could be meant by P, rather than in virtue of C being causally associated with P. Although C is part of what could be meant by P, C by itself may be insufficient to say I is P, for C may be logically independent of P in the sense that a person may say 'This is P but does not have C' or 'This has C but is not P' without contradicting himself or saying something logically false.

To see this in operation again, imagine the following conversation:
A: 'What are they doing?'
B: 'They are on the lawn knocking coloured balls through hoops with wooden mallets.'
A: 'Then they must be playing croquet.'

In this example A's conclusion is not a logical consequence of B's observation, for it is possible to be engaged in a performance which fits this description and yet not be playing croquet: it is possible to use the paraphernalia of croquet to play a different (perhaps novel) game, just as it is possible to play draughts with chessmen. Nevertheless, that

B's observation counts in favour of A's conclusion is something which can be determined without investigating further to find out what game they are playing. For it is not a contingent matter that the description of their action is a description of playing croquet: it is a description of part of the activity which constitutes 'playing croquet', and any full description of the game would refer to action of the kind B described. Moreover, if they were not performing as B described this fact would *count against* the claim that they are playing croquet, even if they are. In short: that they *are* playing croquet is a contingent matter, but that their performance (being what it is) *is a reason* for saying they are playing croquet is a matter of logic.[1] The special position of the connections discussed here can be illustrated in terms of a simple comparative case. The connection between having a rudder and having a funnel is contingent; often the two features are found together and there is no *a priori* linkage between them. It would be correct, in explaining the meaning of 'a rudder', to leave out all mention of funnels. Yet the connection between having a rudder and being *a ship* is not contingent. In explaining the meaning of 'a ship' to someone it would be a serious oversight to omit a mention of the rudder; it is, as we say, a characteristic of a ship. A person who knew nothing of rudders would have a poor and incomplete knowledge of ships, but a person who knew nothing of funnels might have an excellent knowledge of rudders. Yet the connection between having a rudder and being a ship is not a necessary one: there can be at least as many ships without rudders as there are ships washed up on the rocks. The connection is neither necessary nor contingent.

There can be non-necessary *a priori* connections between one statement and another, or between a concept and its characteristics. But a statement to the effect that such a connection obtains is itself a necessary statement.[2] If X is *a priori* a reason for Y, then it is a necessary truth that X is *a priori* a reason for Y. To assert 'X has an eye and a nose is *a priori* a reason in favour of X being a face' is to assert something which, if true, is necessarily true. It is self-contradictory to deny

---

[1] Of course, it is a contingent matter that croquet happens to be played as it is played.

[2] See J. R. Bambrough, 'Principia Metaphysica', *Philosophy*, April 1964, p. 101.

it, just as it is self-contradictory to deny that 'X is smoking a pipe' is *a priori* a reason in favour of 'X is a pipe smoker'. Each of these statements, which asserts that a certain non-necessary connection obtains, is as much a necessary truth as is the assertion that 'X has a St George's cross' is *a priori* a reason in favour of saying 'X is a Union Jack'; although in this case the connection obtaining *is* necessary with so many degrees of freedom.

Of course one might try to preserve the view that concepts are always analytically connected with their characteristics by arguing that if something is of kind K, then necessarily it has either characteristic C_1, or C_2, or . . ., or . . ., specifying a disjunction of characteristics. However this solution forgets that the philosophical motive for maintaining the necessary connection thesis is the hope of finding some identifiable specific feature F necessarily shared by all K's, such that if K, then F. If this must be abandoned the disjunctive view will not do in its place. To say that K's have 'either C_1, or C_2, or . . ., or . . .', so far from determining a particular characteristic which all K's must have, says in effect that no one characteristic, either C_1, or C_2, or . . ., or . . ., is essential to K, and that in any single case the connection between a characteristic and a concept is not necessary. Yet this is the view opposed by the original demand for a necessary connection. The analytic connection between K and its characteristics expressed by the disjunctive view becomes true at the price of being useless; the truism that anything that is of kind K must have some or other characteristic which K's have is hardly informative. Nor will it do to substitute, for the unsatisfactory claim 'If C_n, then K', the argument 'If something has C_1 and C_2 and . . . and . . ., then it is K', specifying a conjunction of all the characteristics of K. It might be held that even if one argues 'If C_1 and C_2 and . . . and . . ., then K' an entailment could not result because the statement of characteristics is indefinite and no list could be given. But there is an even more serious defect, for once again the point of introducing an analytic criterion is undermined. A statement of characteristics entailing K is thought to be required to provide a conclusive test of whether something is, or is not, of kind K, to act as a final court of appeal in deciding cases of K and of not-K. And this is what the attempt to state entailment conditions for K fails to do. In order to ascertain, in the first place, what these conditions are, one must have decided without any such test whether cases are of kind K or not. This is to say that the statement of characteristics which serves as a test of K is itself tested by a procedure which does not appeal to a statement of criteria. The claim 'If C_1 and C_2 and . . . and . . ., then K' is supported or rejected on the grounds of examples known independently to be of kind K and not of kind K. As a result it is unable to do the job it is introduced to accomplish. The peculiarity here is that any statement of the conditions of K may always have to give way to possible exceptions, and it is just this possibility which the appeal to entailment conditions was designed to avoid.

What needs to be resisted is the inclination to think that if a connection is not contingent then it always follows that it is necessary. The demand for *either* a causal connection *or* an entailment in cases where *neither* connection could obtain is one of the major springs of philosophical puzzlement; it persists, perhaps, largely through tradition, for when looked at unfettered by tradition one sees that there is no *need* for the dogma at all, and how it hinders the recognition and exploration of new modes of connection.

4. *The demand for a definition*

SOCRATES: What is piety, and what is impiety?

EUTHRYPHO: Piety is doing what I am doing; that is to say, prosecuting anyone who is guilty of murder, sacrilege, or of any similar crime.

SOCRATES: I would rather hear from you a more precise answer, which you have as yet not given, my friend, to the question, What is 'piety'?

Remember that I did not ask you to give me two or three examples of piety, but to explain the general idea which makes the impious impious, and the pious pious. Tell me what is the nature of this idea, and I shall have a standard to which I may look and by which I may measure an action, and then I shall be able to say that such and such an action is pious, such another impious.

EUTHRYPHO: Piety, then is that which is dear to the gods, and impiety is that which is not dear to them.

SOCRATES: Very good, Euthrypho; you have now given me just the sort of answer which I wanted.[1]

Euthrypho attempts to answer by mentioning a particular case. Socrates believes the question can be answered only by finding an analytic definition. Yet Socrates' own procedure for accepting or rejecting a definition involves exactly the move that he criticizes Euthrypho for making:

Well said, Cephalus, I replied; but as concerning justice, what is it? – to speak the truth and pay your debts – no more than this? And even to this are there not exceptions? Suppose that a friend when in his right mind has deposited arms with me and he asks for them when he is not in his right mind, ought I to give them back to him? No one would say that I ought or that I should be right in doing so, any more than they would say that I ought always to speak the truth to one who is in his condition.

You are quite right, he replied.

But then, I said, speaking the truth and paying your debts is not a correct definition of justice.[2]

Here the standard to which Socrates looks is not, as he recommends, a general definition, but a particular example. Socrates must already know that this action is unjust in order to reject Cephalus' definition. He is right in following a procedure of scrutinizing proposed definitions in the light of possible counter-instances. Before accepting a definition we try to think of cases that support or go against it, and naturally run through in our minds a number of instances to find an exception. This procedure of testing a definition by cases is the common currency of simple and complex argument. But Socrates is wrong in believing that the proper end of his inquiry is a definition admitting no possible exceptions; for the object is to achieve an understanding of the concept at issue and it is not clear that to achieve this one must produce a definition that could not have been false. It is tempting to suppose that Euthrypho's question, or a like question, can be answered *only* in this way, if only because the attempt to find a definition can

[1] Plato, *Euthrypho*, *The Dialogue of Plato*, trs. B. Jowett, New York 1892, Vol. I, 6.
[2] Plato, op. cit., *The Republic*, Book I, 331.

and often does result in the desired understanding. But it is the *search* for a definition that is really valuable here, for it forces one to review the occasions on which the concept applies.

When is a definition useful in philosophy? Perhaps one should first ask, When is a definition useful? A definition of a tetrahedron is useful to a person doing geometry. It is useful to a barrister to know that, necessarily, a burglary takes place at night. This is the *kind* of definition that first strikes one as a sample, and in running through one's thoughts to find examples of definitions in philosophy this kind of case serves as a guide. The inclination to estimate the usefulness of all definitions by comparison with this model is countered by recollecting that not all useful definitions are analytic. To show the exaggerated importance of the analytic model as a paradigm of definition Wittgenstein remarked,

> The idea that in order to get clear about the meaning of a general term one had to find the common element in all its applications, has shackled philosophical investigation; for it has not only led to no result, but has also made the philosopher dismiss as irrelevant the concrete cases, which alone could have helped him to understand the usage of the general term. When Socrates asks the question 'what is knowledge?' he does not even regard it as a *preliminary* answer to enumerate cases of knowledge.[1]

Sometimes Wittgenstein's remarks about the absence of essential common properties are taken to mean that philosophers should break off attempts to search for definitions of those general terms that puzzle them most. It would be a pity if he were understood in this way. For Wittgenstein was trying to combat a 'craving' or 'tendency' in philosophical thinking by putting before us instances that reveal the danger in a tendency to neglect particular cases when habit and philosophical training lead one to look for general definitions. He was not legislating that concepts never have sharp boundaries, but reminding by example that many of the most puzzling ones do not. Nor was he expounding the view that there are *no* concepts which have features necessarily in common to their instances. He was pointing to the mistake of sup-

[1] *The Blue and Brown Books*, pp. 19-20.

posing that all of them must. There is no need to repeat his arguments against the thesis that there must, logically must, be a feature common to all the cases to which any general term applies. Yet there is every need to pay heed to his warning that an attempt to understand the nature of a concept may fail if it is regarded as an attempt to find an exception-proof definition of that concept. A definition that is less than logically true may do, and do better.

In the *Varieties of Religious Experience* William James begins with an argument that is strikingly modern, even Wittgensteinian. If we try to define a word like religion 'we may very likely find no one essence, but many characters which may alternately be equally important in religion . . . there might conceivably also prove to be no one specific and essential kind of religious object, and no one specific and essential kind of religious act.'[1] For all that, James goes on to define what religion is. In this case it is clear that James is not one who has made the mistake Wittgenstein warns against; he does not think for a moment that his definition will satisfy everyone or that no exception could be found. The need is not for a complete inventory of those features whose absence in an instance would be fatal to the application of a concept. There may be no such inventory. Despite this, one may want to present a summary, concise, synoptic and exact view of a concept by defining it. A definition can tell us what features to look for in particular instances without ruling out the possibility of exceptional instances. It can circumscribe the members of a class by specifying what is characteristic of that class though not essential to it. If Euthrypho's definition of piety is incorrect, it is not incorrect because it is not logically true, but because it is inadequate. The merit of a definition is not always that it is logically true or even detailed and precise: it must give us a *grasp* of that which it defines. We speak of an author's description of a character as 'weak' or 'superficial', or say a portrait fails to 'capture the likeness' of the person painted, when they fail to express what is distinctive. Just as there are successful and less-than-successful portraits of a particular person, there are adequate and inadequate definitions of a particular concept. And of course there is more than one good description or good portrait of Waterloo or Wellington. The idea that there can be only a single correct definition

[1] *The Varieties of Religious Experience*, London 1907, pp. 26, 28.

of every concept is as foolish as the idea that there can be only a single good portrait of any person.

Although Wittgenstein warns against an over-emphasis of general definitions which can lead to the neglect of particular cases, we notice that the search for a definition may itself be the means by which particular cases are brought to mind. Even though Socrates looked for a common essence and James did not, both resorted to a definitional procedure with the result that each philosopher made constant reference to the variety of particular instances of the concepts under investigation. It is inconceivable that their inquiries should fail to do this: it is only *from* this range of cases that a definition can be formulated and only *by* them that a definition can be tested.

4

The Problem of Justification

1. *Foreword*

A leading maxim of the traditional theory is that deductive reasoning supplies us with a paradigm to which all our reasoning ought as much as possible to conform. Yet something has gone wrong. For a person X who when asked 'What colour is this cup?' looks at a saucer and says 'This is green' and then looks at the cup and says 'This cup is green' may have as good a reason for his conclusion as does a different person, Y, who looks at the cup and saucer and says 'This saucer is green, this cup is the same colour as the saucer, therefore the cup is green'. There is a tendency to describe the difference between the way X reaches his conclusion, and the way Y reaches his conclusion, by saying that Y has justified or proved his conclusion although X has not; or if this is too strong, then to say that Y has done more than X in the way of giving reasons for his conclusion, for he has reasoned by deduction. True, X and Y have not reasoned in the same way. But is it true that, for instance, a person who looks at X and Y and reasons 'X has less hair than Y and Y is bald, so X is bald since anyone who has less hair than a bald man is also bald' is more justified by his reasoning than is a person who looks at X and at Y and reasons, 'X is bald, so Y is bald'? The answer is no.

The problem of justification is the problem of what counts as a justification and if the wrong models are adopted at the start they will systematically disrupt subsequent inquiry. We can learn a valuable lesson from Moore. He looked no further than the deductive model. He is also a victim of one of the main occupational hazards of philosophers, for his practice is at odds with his preaching. Moore's own practice of reasoning by particulars, we might say *proving* by particulars, is at odds with his belief that he can prove only what he can demonstrate. In spite of this, again and again Moore turns to the direct comparison of one example with another. There is nothing in Moore's work of 'the contemptuous attitude towards the particular case' that Wittgenstein ascribed to philosophers he opposed. Even more than Moore, John Wisdom has emphasized the logical indispensability of reasoning by particular instances; he remarks that 'at the bar of reason always the final appeal is to cases'.[1] This puts the problem of justification and proof in a new and welcome light, and is crucial to an understanding, and a solution, of the complex and interlocking philosophical puzzles that arise when the assumptions of the traditional theory are accepted.

2. Can 'This is an instance of kind K' be justified?

Can a person prove that a predicate applies to a particular case? There is an inclination to say that if one finds the general criteria of a predicate P then one has as much as solved the problem of justifying the application of P to a particular case; for it is possible, given a statement of criteria, to deduce that the case is one of P if the criteria are present. This optimistic proposal may at once be recognized as not meeting the problem, yet it needs to be made plain why it does not.

Let us suppose that a person draws a figure on a blackboard and says, 'This is a pentagon'. Could he thereby justify his statement *simply* by arguing 'This figure has five sides and five angles, and whatever has five sides and as many angles is a pentagon'?[2] By a demonstration alone he would not have established that the figure is a pentagon although it is this that he is called upon to show. Notice first that his statement 'This is a pentagon' is the same sort of statement as 'This is

[1] 'A Feature of Wittgenstein's Technique', *Aristotelian Society Supplementary Volume*, 1961, p. 13.

[2] In all that follows, although an actual instance is presented by the blackboard figure, its actuality is an inessential feature. To review the reasons in a comparable case: People might reach a decision that a certain description describes a voluntary action, without considering at all whether it actually occurred; and the information that it did, or did not, occur would have no bearing on their verdict. To review the principle being used: In questions with regard to the possible, the actual is accidental; and in question with regard to the actual, the consideration of the possible may be the means to the answer.

a cross', or 'This has six letters'; or is of the same sort as 'This is a chair' or even 'This is negligence', which might have been asserted by a person pointing to an object or referring to a description of a situation. It is, then, the same sort of statement as 'This has five sides and five angles', in that each of them predicates a general concept to a particular case. If in support of saying, 'This is a pentagon' a person says 'This has five sides and five angles', he has certainly not established that the figure to which he refers by the word 'this' is a pentagon, nor that the figure to which he refers by the word 'this' has five sides and five angles. So much is obvious: in either case he may have made a mistake, like the mistake made by one who says, 'This is an octagon' of an hexagonal figure drawn on the board. So he has not, clearly, by pointing to the figure on the board and saying the words 'This is a pentagon', shown that the figure is a pentagon and not an octagon. Nor again, if he had said 'A plane figure which has five sides and five angles is a pentagon' would he have established that the figure is a pentagon. So he could not establish that the figure is a pentagon *only* by saying 'This has five sides and five angles' and adding 'if anything has five sides and five angles it is a pentagon'; any more than he could establish the truth of the statement 'This man lied', indicating a particular person, only by saying 'This man intended to deceive me by his words' and adding 'if he intended to deceive me by his words it follows that he lied'. He would have to establish that these propositions are true. And it is not *easy* to see how this can be done.

Now he could not have established the truth of 'This is a pentagon' *only* by arguing thus, although he might have established its truth in this way if he had done something else besides. For, if he had already established 'This figure has five sides and five angles' he could then, in so far as it follows that a plane figure having five sides and five angles is a pentagon, have proved 'This is a pentagon' by deductive inference. But he could not have proved it *unless* he had shown that 'This figure has five sides and five angles' is true, or that some other like statement about the figure on the board which entails 'this is a pentagon' is true. But how is he to show that this figure has five sides and five angles? Or how is he to show that some other like statement, from which it follows that this figure has five sides and five angles and in turn that this figure is a pentagon, is true?

Let us suppose he attempts, as before, to show this by a demonstration: in support of saying 'This figure has five sides and five angles' he says 'This figure has characteristic C_1 and whatever has C_1 has five sides and five angles'. Again, as before, he has done nothing to show that this figure *has* characteristic C_1; this has not been established any more than it had been established that the figure has five sides and five angles. So long as he proceeds in this way there will always be some residual statement of the sort 'This is C_n' or 'This has characteristic C_n,' which has not been established at all, although this statement may be such that if it *had* been established then it would have been proved that this figure is a pentagon. The obvious point, then, is that by a procedure of deduction alone it could not be proved, as in the example when a person points to a blackboard and says 'This is a pentagon' that what he says is correct. But it is possible to show that what he says is correct, by deductive inference, provided some other procedure is adopted in addition.

The difficulty of establishing the propositions that need to be established becomes at this point acute, for having eliminated deduction it is clear that in the circumstances it will not do to fall back on the reply that we need now only conduct empirical investigations. For all the investigation that needs to be done has been done, and we are not in the position of someone who says there was a pentagon here yesterday, or will be tomorrow, or that there is one now on the board though half-covered by a map. The conclusion is that on an occasion in which further observation is beside the point, even reasoning carried out deductively is not by itself sufficient to prove that a case is one of a certain kind. A procedure of reasoning other than deduction must be found.

3. *Moore's proof*

Is Moore a sceptic? At first sight it seems the answer must be 'No', for Moore has said he can prove what a sceptic doubts, that two human hands exist. But there is a reason why it might be right to answer 'Yes, a sceptic about proof'. It is worth bringing out why this answer might be right and how it throws new light on Moore's technique and on the concept of proof itself.

Presenting his proof of an external world Moore says,

> I can prove now, for instance, that two human hands exist, How?
> By holding up my two hands, and saying, as I make a certain ges-
> ture with the right hand, 'Here is one hand', and adding, as I make
> a certain gesture with the left, 'and here is another'.[1]

What kind of argument does Moore use in his proof? This proof,
Moore says, is required to meet three conditions. First, that the premise 'Here is one hand and here is another' together with certain ges-
tures, is different from the conclusion; secondly that the premise was
something Moore knew to be the case and not something which he
only believed or thought was so; and thirdly that the conclusion 'Two
human hands exist at this moment' did follow logically from the premise. Obviously, then, Moore's proof amounts to a demonstration:
there is a deductive inference from the premise 'Here is one hand and
here is another' to the conclusion 'At least two human hands exist'.
Notice Moore insists that his proof would not be a proof unless he
knew for certain that 'Here is one hand and here is another' is true; if
he did not know this, he thinks, the claim 'At least two human hands
exist' would not follow. It is essential to his proof that he does know
this, since it cannot be the case that he both knows that here is one
hand and here is another and that this proposition is false; that is, if
he knows 'Here is one hand and here is another' then this proposition
is true and any proposition which follows from it, e.g. 'At least two
human hands exist', is also true. Moore's argument is simply this:
Here is one hand and here is another, therefore at least two human
hands exist.

The second thing to notice is that although Moore insists he has
proved the conclusion he also insists that he has *not* proved the proposition which is his premise, 'Here is one hand and here is another'.
He says he does not think a proof of this proposition could be given.
Now it seems important to find out just *why* Moore says he cannot
prove 'Here is one hand and here is another', even though he says he
can prove his conclusion that two human hands exist.

The first reason is that Moore believes that any proof of a proposition must involve a premise; if he is to prove that 'Here is one hand and

[1] *Philosophical Papers*, London 1959, pp. 145-6.

here is another' he must have some premise in the proof, in the same way in which he had this proposition as a premise for the proof of 'At least two human hands exist'. One reason, then, why Moore says he cannot prove 'Here is one hand and here is another' is that he believes he could not give a proof of this without a premise and also that, in this case, he cannot give any such premise. Now undoubtedly this proposition might follow logically from *some* premise, but that premise would itself either follow from no premise at all, or follow logically from some still further premises one of which, ultimately, does not follow from any premise; this regress comes to a stop if, as Moore thinks, any one of these premises is known to be true, a point Moore consistently emphasizes throughout his work: 'It must be the case that we are capable of knowing at least *one* proposition to be true, *without* knowing any other proposition whatever from which it follows'.[1] Yet to say a proposition is true because it follows from some other proposition which is known to be true, and to say a proposition is true because it is known to be true, are according to Moore two very different things: in the first case, if a proposition is a logical consequence of some other proposition known to be true then that proposition, in virtue of its being a logical consequence of a proposition known to be true, has been proved to be true; in the second case, although the proposition is known to be true it has not, in virtue of this alone, been proved to be true: it does not follow from the evidence for asserting it. It is Moore's view that if a proposition is to be proved it must be deduced from some premise.

We should be struck by the fact that Moore thinks he cannot prove his premise 'Here is one hand and here is another' for the very reasons which a sceptic gives for doubting that this premise can be known. In the first place Moore thinks he cannot prove he is not dreaming:

How am I to prove now that 'Here's one hand, and here's another'? I do not believe I can do it. In order to do it, I should need to prove for one thing, as Descartes pointed out, that I am not now dreaming. But how can I prove that I am not? I have, no doubt, conclusive reasons for asserting that I am not now dreaming; I have conclusive evidence that I am awake: but that is a very different

[1] *Some Main Problems of Philosophy*, London 1953, p. 123.

thing from being able to prove it. I could not tell you what all my evidence is; and I should require to do this at least, in order to give you a proof.[1]

It is not precisely clear from Moore's brief passage why he says he cannot prove he is not at the moment dreaming. By saying, 'I could not tell you what all my evidence is', which he gives as the only reason for saying he could not give a proof, he seems to mean that he could not construct a premise from which it would *follow logically* that he is not dreaming; he seems to be suggesting that his evidence is always incomplete, that further evidence could always be relevant. And this is consistent with his view that if he is to prove he is not dreaming, he must demonstrate that he is not. For the incompleteness of his evidence would preclude a demonstration. The interesting thing about this passage is its similarity to an argument which Russell has frequently given to cast doubt on the possibility of a person's knowing he is awake and not dreaming: 'I do not believe that I am now dreaming, but I cannot prove that I am not. I am, however, quite certain that I am having certain experiences, whether they be those of a dream or those of waking life'.[2] Russell's point in this argument is that the evidence of a person's sensations from which he infers on some occasions that he is not dreaming, and on other occasions that he is, is not such that, were the evidence stated, it would follow logically that he is not dreaming, or that he is. Whether this is exactly the same as the point of Moore's argument may be debated, for unfortunately Moore does not say enough. There is some reason to suppose it is not exactly the same argument. For Moore's argument seems to be that, because he can never complete a statement of all the evidence from which it would follow that he is not dreaming, proof of this is impossible. Whereas Russell seems to be saying, in this passage, that no matter how much evidence a person has or could have to conclude he is not dreaming, whatever the amount it consists entirely of his immediate sensory experiences, and as such any statement of this evidence is logically compatible either with the conclusion that his experiences are those of a dream, or that they are not. Yet it is clear that both

---

[1] *Philosophical Papers*, p. 149.
[2] *Human Knowledge*, London 1948, p. 186.

Moore and Russell agree that *some*, if not exactly the same, argument shows that such a thing as that I am not now dreaming cannot be proved. And the object of the argument is to establish that the common sense conclusion that I am not now dreaming is not a logical consequence of my immediate experiences. But they disagree in one important respect: while Moore would allow he can know he is not dreaming, without being able to prove it, this is a concession which Russell refuses to make.

Notice also that Moore assents to a sceptic's arguments in his paper, 'Four Forms of Scepticism'. Moore represents Russell as arguing that a man cannot know for certain that a pencil is before him, or cannot know for certain that other people are conscious, and reaching this conclusion on the assumption that 'This is a pencil' and 'That person is conscious' are neither *i*. known immediately, nor *ii*. follow logically from anything a person does know immediately, that *iii*. if *i* and *ii* are true, knowledge of them is reached by inductive or analogical inference, and *iv*. that such inference cannot result in certain knowledge. Russell's argument here is not very different from his previous one about dreaming: the principle is that the inference from things each of which a person knows immediately to conclusions not immediately known by anyone is never deductive, and being an inductive inference or an analogical argument, yields conclusions which no one can know with certainty. This is a standard form of sceptical argument. But look at Moore's reply to it:

> Is it, in fact, as certain that all these four assumptions are true, as that I *do* know that this is a pencil and that you are conscious? I cannot help answering: It seems to me *more* certain that I *do* know that this is a pencil and that you are conscious, than that any single one of these four assumptions is true, let alone all four. That is to say, though, as I have said, I agree with Russell that *i*, *ii* and *iii* *are* true; yet of no one even of these three do I feel *as* certain as that I do know for certain that this is a pencil.

And a bit earlier on:

> I cannot help agreeing with Russell that I never know immediately such a thing as 'That person is conscious' or 'This is a pencil',

and that also the truth of such propositions never follows logically from anything which I do know immediately, and yet I think that I do know such things for certain.[1]

In both this argument of Russell's and the previous one about dreaming the chief sceptical move is to show the lack of a necessary connection between evidence and conclusions: that the conclusion 'I am not dreaming right now' does not follow logically from my immediate sensory experience or from statements about such experience; that the conclusion 'This is a pencil' or 'That person is conscious' cannot be deduced from the immediate evidence for asserting it. I want especially to call attention to the fact that Moore *does not disagree* with these premises from which Russell derived his doubts; he disagrees only with Russell's conclusion. The issue between Moore and a sceptic comes to this: Moore declares he can know such a thing as 'Here is one hand and here is another' or 'This is a pencil' without being able to prove it deductively from some premise, while a sceptic argues that, lacking deductive proof, Moore cannot claim to have such knowledge. Is there any reason to say that Moore is really a sceptic? Surely the fact that he accepts a sceptic's arguments, although rejecting a sceptic's conclusions, is insufficient. But the conclusion he rejects is that no one can *know* any such propositions as he mentions, and while this would count against saying Moore is a sceptic about knowledge it does not count against saying Moore is a sceptic about *proof*.

On page 75 of *Principia Ethica* Moore says that 'in certain cases proof is impossible':

> For instance, nobody can prove that this is a chair beside me; yet I do not suppose that anyone is much dissatisfied for that reason. We all agree that it is a chair, and that is enough to content us, although it is quite possible we may be wrong. A madman, of course might come in and say that it is not a chair but an elephant. We could not prove that he was wrong, and the fact that he did not agree with us might then begin to make us uneasy.

This paradoxical passage seems out of character in Moore's work and more at home in Russell's scepticism. For surely it is common sense to suppose a person can prove he is not sitting on an elephant when he is sitting on a chair, although perhaps not immediately plain how it is to be proved. Just as Moore has often asserted that all of us know many things although we do not know *how* we know them it might be expected in the present case Moore would argue that although there are many things, such as the fact that a person is sitting on a chair, which any of us might have been able to prove, they are such that we do not know how to explain the method of proof. Yet this is not Moore's argument; he *denies* that any proof exists. He is not saying merely that we do not understand how such proof might proceed. He does this in much the same way in which a sceptic denies we know such things as that there are chairs and tables. It is not always recognized how close Moore's philosophy is to the sceptical doctrines he consistently opposed, for the clash between Moore and a sceptic takes place over the application of the concepts of existence and knowledge. But when we pass on to the concept of proof Moore's work changes its colour: following a sceptic's lead Moore identifies conclusive proof with logical demonstration and refuses to allow that anyone is able to prove things which he is unable to demonstrate. We see this in his contention that he can prove his conclusion that at least two material things exist because this follows logically from the premise that he has two hands, but that the premise itself cannot be proved. When fundamental questions about the proof of a proposition arise, there is reason to call Moore a sceptic.

Let us look at one of Moore's most familiar arguments. He has often maintained that various common sense propositions are *more* certain than a philosophical principle supporting conclusions which go against them, and that therefore the principle must be false. One well-known example is his statement 'I know this pencil exists; therefore Hume's principles are false'; Hume's argument, he says, is 'a characteristic instance of a sort of argument which is very common in philosophy: namely, an attempt to prove that a given proposition is false, by means of a principle which is, in fact, much less certain than the proposition which is supposed to be proved false by its means'.[1]

One would expect that if Moore is to be consistent he would say it is more certain that one might prove it is a chair and not an elephant

[1] *Some Main Problems of Philosophy*, p. 143.

beside him, though perhaps not knowing how to prove it, than that a philosophical principle to the effect that such a proposition cannot be proved is true. But he does not. At this point Moore discards his familiar procedure and adopts the same type of argument which he says is so common in philosophy and which he thinks is certainly mistaken, for he believes that the proposition that a person might prove it is a chair and not an elephant which is beside him is false, simply because he believes the principle that nothing is a conclusive proof unless it is a demonstration, is true.

Despite this principle, on occasions Moore resorts to a technique of non-demonstrative argument which he believes supports certain claims he makes, such as that his proof of an external world really is a proof. This technique is obvious and easy to understand as soon as one sees it employed; it is apt to go unnoticed because of its simplicity and because it very closely resembles, although is different from, Moore's procedure of using a counter-instance against a sceptic's general statement. It is a form of argument by analogy perhaps best described as argument by parallel or comparable cases. I want to show how Moore uses this argument and that it is a kind of reasoning which might, in the absence of a deductive proof, establish just those propositions Moore said he could not prove.

It is necessary to see that Moore uses particular cases in two distinct and different ways. On some occasions he uses a particular case (let us call this 'use *a*') as a means of showing that some general statement or principle is false. If a philosopher says there can be no proof of the existence of things outside of us, Moore might reply by presenting an example of such a proof; if it is said that no such things as human hands exist, Moore might gesture, indicate his hands and say 'But here are hands'. This use of particular instances is the one we associate with Moore's familiar technique of presenting a particular counter-instance to a philosopher's sceptical conclusion. It has the immediate effect of bringing out the paradoxicality of a sceptic's conclusion even if we allow it does not refute it, for it is often thought that by presenting a single case Moore has not refuted the general assertion and has done nothing to justify his claim. It seems as if he has begged the question. The second way in which Moore uses particular cases (call this 'use *b*') often goes on to refer to other cases analogous to the one he first mentions. He appeals, in use *b*, to parallel cases; and the reason he does this, as will be clear from his text, is to secure some justification for the original case he presents as a counter-instance to a sceptic's general claim. For example: Suppose a sceptic says motion is impossible; to this Moore might reply, 'But motion *is* possible: look, I am moving my hand from my lap to my head, so what you say cannot be true'. Here he is using a case as in *a*. But he might go on to strengthen his claim that he was moving his hand by continuing to argue in the following manner: 'If you say that I did not move my hand, you might as well say I am not now moving my feet when I cross them like this, or that I am not now moving this book from the table to the floor, thusly, or that this book was not just then moved from the table to the floor'. Here he is using cases as in *b*. That the use of cases here is not the same as in the previous example is clear, first from the obvious fact that two or more cases are necessarily involved if there is to be a comparison or parallelism, while only one of them would be enough to challenge a sceptic's statement; and, secondly, the use of additional cases is not merely gratuitous but in the same way *supports* the reply 'But I am moving my hand from my lap to my head'. And in use *b* each of the cases is different from the other, enabling a person to argue from one case to another, e.g. '*This* is a case of movement, and so is *that*; so isn't this other instance a case of movement too?'

Two preliminary examples illustrate Moore's use of this procedure. In his 'Proof of an External World' Moore's reply to the objection that he did not know at the time that he gestured with his hands, is as follows:

> How absurd it would be to suggest that I did not know it, but only believed it, and that perhaps it was not the case! You might as well suggest that I do not know that I am now standing up and talking – that perhaps after all I'm not, and that it's not quite certain that I am![1]

In trying to show that it is absurd to doubt he knew he raised his hands Moore makes reference to a parallel case of an absurdity. Whether this particular argument in which he appeals to an analogous case is a good argument, or whether any other arguments of the same kind are ever good arguments, will have to be decided. At any rate it is

[1] *Philosophical Papers*, pp. 146-147.

clear Moore thinks that by mentioning a comparable case he is strengthening his claim about the original case and that this reasoning has some force. For he makes use of it again immediately after this passage:

> And finally it was quite certain that the conclusion did follow from the premise. This is as certain as it is that if there is one hand here and another here *now*, then it follows that there are two hands in existence *now*.

Again the procedure of reasoning comes to paralleling one case with another.

A reading of his text shows that this procedure of appealing to analogous or parallel instances constitutes the main argument which Moore gives to establish that his proof of an external world really is a proof. It seemed important to Moore that he should in some way justify his claim that he did prove, when he gestured with his hands, that two human hands were then in existence, and not merely insist that he gave a proof. He is, or course, certain that he did prove this. He says that his argument satisfies three of the conditions necessary for a rigorous proof, which he mentions: that the premise is different from the conclusion, that the premise was something he knew to be the case, and that the conclusion did follow logically from the premise. And although Moore makes it plain that his proof would not have been a proof unless these three conditions were satisfied, he asks, 'Are there any other conditions necessary for a rigorous proof, such that perhaps it did not satisfy one of them? Perhaps there may be', Moore says, 'I do not know.' Moore is not claiming that these three conditions are the only conditions which a rigorous proof must satisfy; he is not arguing that his proof is a proof because it satisfies these three conditions, but only that if it failed to satisfy them he would not have proved his conclusion. For one thing, Moore explicitly gives further argument to show that his proof really *is* a proof, and his reasoning comes to no more than the mention of a similar case:

> Suppose, for instance, it were a question whether there were as many as three misprints on a certain page in a certain book. A says there are, B is inclined to doubt it. How could A prove that he is right? Surely he *could* prove it by taking the book, turning to the page, and

pointing to three separate places on it, saying, 'There's one misprint here, another here, and another here': surely that is a method by which it *might* be proved! Of course, A would not have proved, by doing this, that there were at least three misprints on the page in question, unless it was certain that there was a misprint in each of the places to which he pointed. But to say that he *might* prove it in this way, is to say that it *might* be certain that there was. And if such a thing as that could ever be certain, then assuredly it was certain just now that there was one hand in one of the two places I indicated and another in the other.[1]

Has this form of reasoning any force? Of course Moore might have given an analogous case different from the one which he did give, or he might have given several such cases: there is no need to limit the number of parallel instances to which he could have made reference. But even if he had made reference to still further cases the question still remains whether by this procedure he gives any justification. The very fact that Moore does at some length and in detail mention this second case as supporting his proof that there were two hands, convincingly shows he believes it to play a justificatory role. Clearly this argument by parallels is *in favour* of his point, and therefore this type of argument is one which might have been used in favour of a great many other points. The question is how much force we should allow it to have.

Moore himself has not answered this question, but it is fairly clear that he would not allow this argument to constitute a proof. For it is a form of argument which he gives in situations where he has said no proof is available; for example, he uses it in the passage just quoted to show that 'Here is one hand and here is another' was certain, but he does not think this could ever be proved. And by saying he can give no proof of it Moore has in mind that, although he can know it is true, he cannot prove it deductively. Nevertheless he has argued in its favour by means of a parallel case, so this reasoning seems to be a form of argument which might be used when deduction is ruled out and yet where some argument is required. Inductive argument seems the natural alternative, but we should not suppose that argument by parallels must

[1] *Philosophical Papers*, p. 147.

be the same as induction. Indeed it can differ from induction in at least one fundamental respect: the cases to which reference is made in support need not record anything which has actually happened, or is thought to have actually happened, but only something which might have happened, even if it did not, and even if it is thought not to have happened. Moore's case of the misprints is itself hypothetical: he argues that it *might* be proved there are three misprints on a certain page, and that the premise from which this follows might be certain. Clearly an inductive argument cannot be based on possible, hypothetical or fictional cases, if its aim is to yield conclusions or hypotheses about what actually is so. In an argument by parallels actual or fictional examples have equal authority in so far as they support a claim about what is possible. It is probably true that Moore himself regarded his appeal to cases as a way of referring to actual empirically verified instances, even though he sometimes gave merely possible cases.[1] Nevertheless there is no need to elaborate this distinction for our present purpose, for Moore by restricting the title of conclusive proof to a demonstration excludes inductive arguments as well as justification by parallel cases. It is this latter form of reasoning which he employs when he allows, as we have seen, a sceptic's arguments to preclude the possibility of proving a conclusion which he says he knows is certain. We may think that Moore is a sceptic about proof because in situations where a deductive proof cannot be given he refused to allow that a proof of some other kind is possible. The question is, therefore, whether Moore's technique of appealing to parallel cases *might* be a way of providing the needed justification under these circumstances.

But we must first decide whether it is true that a proposition which cannot be proved by deduction cannot be proved at all. Let us take the proposition whose proof Moore doubted, 'Here is one hand, and here is another' and call it proposition P. In the context of our discussion a philosopher who says 'P cannot be proved by deduction' means that P cannot be deduced from premises about the immediate evidence for asserting it. Now from the proposition 'Proposition P cannot be proved by deduction' by itself, it does not follow logically that P could not have been proved in some other way. It does not follow from this proposition alone that it is false that P might have been

[1] See, for instance, *Some Main Problems of Philosophy*, pp. 142–43.

proved, just as that from this proposition alone it does not follow, as Moore has argued, that no one might have known P is true. Of course, it would follow that P could not be proved to be true if P were false, or that P could not be proved to be false if P were true; but P is such that, if it were true, it might have been false, and if false might have been true; so it is possible to say that P might have been proved to be true for P might have been true, or that P might have been false for P might have been false. Most certainly it is not self-contradictory to say 'Proposition P cannot be proved by deduction from the immediate evidence for asserting it, although P might have been proved in some other way'; the mere fact that an argument is not a demonstration does not entail that the argument is not a proof. Even if it were true to say that an argument which is not a logical demonstration is not a proof, this would not be a logical consequence of the proposition 'Proposition P cannot be proved by deduction'. In order to show that this proposition is true something else would have to be done. And of course, 'Proposition P cannot be proved by deduction' does not entail that P *could* be proved by any means whatever. Doubtless it will be said that the meaning of the word 'proof' is such that if anything is a proof it necessarily involves a premise, a conclusion and a necessary connection between them. But surely the word 'proof' is not *always* so used; nor if used in any other way is it, on that account alone, used incorrectly. By so restricting the word 'proof' we tend to suppose also that the words 'conclusive justification' or 'conclusive reasons' are similarly restricted to apply only to demonstrations: and that if a person said that such and such were conclusive reasons for P, or that they conclusively established P, he would have to mean that P was a logical consequence of these reasons. This restriction, even more than the restriction upon the use of the word 'proof', seems doubtful; for it *might* make sense to say either *a*. 'P is not a logical consequence of reasons R, although R conclusively establishes P' or *b*. 'P cannot be proved although P can be conclusively established on the grounds of R' when 'prove' is being used to mean 'demonstrate'. For one thing, it might make sense to say this in the following circumstances: when P cannot be demonstrated on the grounds of R, not merely because an attempted demonstration is invalid, but because no proposition of the kind of which P is an instance *could* follow logically from any proposition, or propositions, of the kind of which R is an instance. For example *i*. from the proposition 'There is one person on the chair and another person on the sofa' it does not follow logically that 'There are at least three people on the furniture', although a different conclusion of the same kind, 'There are at least two people on the furniture' would follow. But *ii*. from the proposition 'There *seems* to be one person on the chair and another on the sofa' neither of these conclusions follow. In both examples there was an invalid inference, but in the second example, unlike the first, it is impossible to alter the conclusion (or the premise) of the invalid inference to get a valid inference without also altering the kind of proposition. In the first example you could not say of any inference that it is invalid simply from knowing that the premise and conclusion are both the same kind of statement: for instance, that both of them are known immediately, or that both are not known immediately; whereas in the second example, according to Moore, you *could* say whether the inference is invalid simply from knowing that the premise and conclusion are not of the same kind, that, for instance, the premise is something which is known immediately while the conclusion is not known immediately. For we have Moore's judgement that he cannot prove propositions like 'Here is a pencil' or 'That person is conscious' for he allows, as we have noted, that propositions of this kind are not known immediately and none of them follow from any other propositions, of a different kind, which are known immediately. He accepts a sceptic's thesis that there is no necessary connection between a proposition expressing the immediate evidence for saying such a thing as 'Here is a pencil', and the proposition 'Here is a pencil'. In *this* situation it might make sense to say that a proposition like 'Here is a pencil' could be conclusively established even though it cannot be proved by deduction from some ultimate premise; because if we say, in this situation, that P cannot be proved deductively we are saying that no proposition whatsoever of the kind of which P is an instance can be proved deductively and not merely that a particular proposition P cannot be proved: we are *not* saying, for example, merely that P does not follow from R because it violates the rules of inference, but *are* saying that P does not follow from R because the inference is invalid for the reason that no propositions of the kind to which P belongs *could* follow logically from any propositions of the kind to which R belongs, which is a very different thing. And if this is true it is necessarily true; *if* it is true it is a necessary characteristic of all propositions like 'Here's a pencil' – none of them could be demonstrated on the grounds of the immediate evidence for asserting them. In this situation nothing is allowed to count as a possible proof of *any* proposition of this kind.

Yet it is obviously paradoxical to say that a person could never prove that he is holding up a pencil. A man who says it is impossible for me or anyone else to prove that I live in such and such a place, such and such a house, have a car, or a watch in my pocket, or even that I have two arms and two legs, is saying something which would certainly be doubted at the level of common sense. It is commonly accepted that each of these things might be proved in a court of law. Our ordinary use of the word 'proof' is not restricted only to what we can demonstrate. It *makes sense* for me to say that I can prove that today is Sunday, simply by pointing to today's newspapers, to the fact that people are going to church and the shops are shut, and to an indefinite number of other pieces of evidence. This would be a perfectly good proof, and I could so present my case that it would be accepted as conclusively showing today is Sunday. No doubt it will be thought that my conclusion that today is Sunday is finally based on the evidence of things which I know immediately and that I do not know immediately that today is Sunday, and therefore this conclusion does not logically follow. But even if this is admitted, it is far more paradoxical to say that I could not prove in some such way that today is Sunday and to say no one ever could prove it, that no one ever could prove what day of the week it is today, than to say such a thing *might* be proved. The very absurdity of the thesis makes it astonishing that Moore should have accepted it. To doubt that any of these things might be proved is surely to express a scepticism as paradoxical as the scepticism about knowledge which Moore himself opposed. If there is any good reason for Moore's scepticism about proof it should derive from the fact that no way of proving propositions of this or of any kind seems available once deduction is excluded.

Nevertheless, Moore has himself shown by his own practice that there is a further procedure, one which can be used to justify propositions for which deductive reasons ultimately cannot be given: we have seen him give reasons for a conclusion of the form 'This is K' by reasoning from comparable cases.

4. *The ultimate appeal is to instances*

John Wisdom has convincingly expounded and elaborated the thesis that the comparison of cases is fundamental to knowledge, and brought to life the importance and logical force of argument by instances in a way in which Moore never did. It is difficult to give an account that does justice to the subtility and scope of Wisdom's views. He has argued that all reasoning calls for comparison, and of all the philosophical truths that need to be understood this is the one of widest scope. To come to know that a thing is of a certain kind is to come to know what it is *like*; to claim that a thing is of a certain kind is to claim that it parallels other things of that kind. The word 'parallels' suggests both a likeness and a difference, and by making plain what these parallels are, if only by setting out particular cases side by side, a person may justify his claim. The most direct way of bringing support to bear is to use the simple technique of calling attention to likenesses and differences between the case at issue and other actual or possible cases. The emphasis is on reasoning by the comparison of cases as a *direct* procedure involving no intervening premises or inferences. Deduction, in contrast, is an *indirect* procedure, a means of bringing one case to bear on another by the use of a general premise 'showing a track through the manifold of cases' (Wisdom). The procedure of direct reasoning is not intended to supersede other, indirect, methods. In principle, though not in practice, indirect methods are dispensable. But the direct procedure is logically fundamental: anyone who appeals directly to cases can give *as good* a justification for what he says as can anyone who argues by deduction.

In all of this Wisdom is pointing to a new dimension of reasoning and proof. If the leading slogan is that the comparison of particulars is fundamental to knowledge, its basis lies in the intimate connection between justification and understanding. To prove a proposition is not merely to give an argument but to reason in a way that brings comprehension and conviction. And in this there is a connection between Wisdom's thesis and Wittgenstein's claim that a proof must be perspicuous; the reasoning must not only be conclusive, it must be seen to be. Wisdom describes the following case: 'A child asks, "What is a greyhound?" His father replies, "A greyhound is a dog of a certain sort". "I know", says the child, "but what sort?" "Well", his father says, "a greyhound is a dog in which the power to weight ratio . . ." But his mother interrupts. "Look", she says, "that's a greyhound, and you remember your Uncle's dog, Entry Badge, well that was a greyhound. But now that", she says, pointing to a Borzoi, "is not a greyhound, and even that", she says, pointing to a whippet, "is not" . . . In short the mother replies with instances of what is and what is not a greyhound or by comparing greyhounds with what they are not, and these two procedures merge into one.'[1] There is an inclination to describe the difference between the way the father answers the child and the way the mother answers by saying that the father began to give conclusive reasons to the child while the mother did not; for he has stated a definition, a general premise which one might use in a proof, while the mother has mentioned no premises or definitions but only instances. Wisdom warns us of the danger of this inclination. On the contrary, by setting out case by case things that are greyhounds and things that are not, mother's reply can be *no less* conclusive than father's.

Sometimes we think that the reasons we have for saying 'This is a so and so' or 'That is such and such' are insecure unless we can lay down a list of criteria. We feel we must get *outside* the instances themselves to avoid circularity and that we do not finally derive reason from particular cases but from a general specification or definition, having the role of a yardstick by which we measure a case at issue. Its use is to serve as an independent guarantee that our judgement is right. But how is this independent guarantee itself supported? The answer is, by looking at the concrete cases to which the specification refers. This is concealed by the fact that our intention in finding general criteria is often to distinguish between particular cases of different kinds, and the illusion is created that this process is the ultimate justificatory procedure. But the general standard is itself justified in terms of particular cases. The move which escapes us is that when we demand a general statement of criteria to judge particular cases, we overlook that we also

[1] 'The Metamorphosis of Metaphysics', *Proceedings of The British Academy*, 1961, p. 48.

use particular cases to test, confirm or discredit the statement of criteria. Let us be clear about this: propositions about the general features of concepts are arrived at and supported by the consideration of particular instances. Since the individual instances are the grounds we finally have for formulating or rejecting a general definition, no change simply in the logical form of their presentation, e.g. presenting them in terms of a definition, can make the instances less certain than the definition itself. A general proposition can have no more certainty than the particular instances on which it is based. Although appeal to a general definition may as a matter of fact guide us in a reliable, swift and comprehensible way in the identification of a concept, it does not as a matter of logic impart to the results it yields a greater certainty than that yielded by the results of inquiry involving no more than the direct comparison of cases. It is Wisdom's belief that the direct comparison of cases can be used when inductive and deductive methods fail. They may fail when a person tries to justify a proposition like 'This is a hand', 'This is knowledge' or even 'This is red', as we have seen.

They may fail also when one tries to justify a law of logic, a rule of logical inference or an ultimate logical premise. Aristotle has remarked that it is impossible that there should be a demonstration of absolutely everything, for there would be an infinite regress and so some things must remain undemonstrated. With this in mind, it appears that since any chain of deductions must begin with something undefended by deductions, a point will be reached where an ultimate premise or principle stands on its own as being intuitively clear or self-evident. And to say that a proposition is 'self-evident' is to say in effect that no reasons can be given on its behalf, leaving it incapable of proof. This result seems, and is, unsatisfactory. For even if a proposition is said to be 'self-evident' this does not preclude the possibility of its rational support. The question is how it can be supported. Perhaps one will think that the regress to which Artistotle points results from not distinguishing between a premise and a rule of inference, and that the statement of the rule stands apart from the inference as an independent means of justification. This, to put it mildly, is a dodge: for the authority exerted over the inference is exactly the same whether the statement is construed as a 'rule' or a 'premise', and both are equally vulnerable to question. The problem at the moment is whether anything

better can be said in support of a high-level logical principle than that
it is incapable of justification.

To take a case, how could the law of contradiction be defended?
One answer is to look at the way it might be taught or explained to
someone who does not understand. Russell does this in *The Problems
of Philosophy*, where he explains the law first by stating it and then by
giving examples:

> Let us take as an illustration the law of contradiction. This is
> commonly stated in the form 'Nothing can both be and not be',
> which is intended to express the fact that nothing can at once have
> and not have a given quality. Thus, for example, if a tree is a beech
> it cannot also be not a beech; if my table is rectangular it cannot
> also be not rectangular, and so on.[1]

In this passage it is Russell's intention to instruct his readers. Yet he
is not doing merely that, for he is giving as well an argument that
supports the law. He might have *concluded* from the examples he cites
that the law is as he states it. Most certainly they are more than convenient illustrations. They are *reasons* for the law being what it is, or,
one might say, there is no better reason than these and the comparable
cases indicated by the words 'and so on'. By mentioning examples
Russell is defending the law by appealing to the ultimate evidence for
asserting it, and obviously this defence is not itself a deduction, or a
procedure of inductive reasoning.

Russell is led to believe that the law of contradiction cannot be defended by argument ('Some at least of these principles must be granted
before any argument or proof becomes possible') partly through a
failure to see that this elementary procedure of teaching is a primitive
procedure of proof, and partly because he (mistakenly) supposes that
an appeal to particular instances is a form of inductive inference. In
his eyes, accordingly, it is no method of argument, since he has pre-
viously eliminated both induction and deduction as legitimate justificatory methods for logical laws and principles. He is forced to conclude
that the notion of proof does not apply to them. The unsatisfactori-
ness of Russell's attempt to give an account of the nature of logical
appraisal lies in the erroneous dogma through which he sees the prob-

[1] Pp. 136–37.

lems rather than in his actual practice. For he adds, 'It is usually through particular instances that we come to see the general principle', and with this Russell had provided all the pieces we need. He is right in claiming that the inductive and deductive models are inappropriate. He is also right in emphasizing the role of the comparison of cases in coming to know the meaning of a logical principle. In fact in this quotation he is giving us a view about the way in which logical principles *are* defended, rather than a view of why they cannot be defended. But he has not seen that by his procedure of explaining the meaning of a logical principle by reference to its instances he is also setting out, instance by instance, the grounds for accepting the principle at all. To do this is to reason directly and conclusively.

Let us see why reflective reasoning by the direct comparison of instances is not inductive argument. In an inductive argument a person, in effect, bets on the existence of a striking analogy between observed cases and a case at issue on the grounds of the observed presence of less striking analogy. For example, he may argue by induction 'There is clockwork inside this toy for it moves when wound up', and give as his reasons a variety of actual cases of analogous performance found on investigation to contain clockwork. But in the type of argument from instances which we have been considering, no inference is made to unobserved data on the evidence of observed data. If in settling the application of a concept to a case inductive inference plays a role, its part is antecedent to deliberative reasoning. The crucial factor of difference lies in the peculiarity that possible and not merely actual cases are enlisted in argument by direct comparison, though rejected by induction in favour of the records of actual observation.

Thus, reasoning by the appreciation of parallels, in virtue of its use of imaginary cases, differs from Mill's view that all inference is ultimately from particulars to particulars. Although Mill held that in drawing inferences we most often conclude from particulars to particulars directly rather than through the indirect agency of a general proposition, and that a general proposition is logically dispensable in an inference, serving as a 'kind of shorthand' of the particular instances, he had in mind that by such reasoning one proceeds from observed to unobserved cases. His work is an attempt to establish induction as the primary form of reasoning to which all other forms of

F

reasoning may be reduced. He did not represent this type of reasoning as wholly reflective, but as involving inferences from past instances to those anticipated in the future, 'from facts certified by observation to facts which we have not observed'.[1] Nevertheless it will be obvious that much of what is said here is in agreement with Mill's view; especially his belief that the proof of a proposition does not finally rest upon a general principle but on the particular instances falling under that principle, some of which, at least, are instances of the proposition to be proved by means of deduction from the principle. This consideration led Mill to assert that every syllogism is a *petitio principii* and that no proof is possible so long as reasoning is confined to passing from generals to particulars. By doing this Mill was not questioning the validity of syllogistic reasoning but maintaining that the syllogism conceals the type of inference actually employed; that the inference does not proceed from a universal proposition to a particular instance, though does proceed from the instances upon which the universal proposition is based to a conclusion about a particular case.

Traditionally an argument is said to be circular if, when A implies B, B is used to prove A by being part of the evidence on which A is based, and in turn A is used to prove B since B is a logical consequence of A. This does not, however, make the point of Mill's conclusion. In his theory of the syllogism Mill asked how we come to know the major premise 'All men are mortal'. We learn this, he says, by enumeration of instances of the death of particular men, and from those instances which have been observed we infer a conclusion, 'All men are mortal', including observed and unobserved cases. It can be deduced that a living man, Mill's example is the Duke of Wellington, is mortal, and clearly this instance is not part of the evidence used to establish the premise 'All men are mortal'. Here Mill differs from the traditional view, for he is not asserting that the syllogism is circular because the conclusion is part of the evidence establishing the major premise, but rather that the evidence for the conclusion is the same as the evidence for the major premise. Mill's point is that, from the evidence of particular instances of mortality, we are equally entitled to infer 'The Duke of Wellington is mortal' as 'All men are mortal': we may conclude directly that the Duke of Wellington is mortal, without interposing

[1] *A System of Logic*, Bk. II, ch. 1, sec. 3.

the major premise 'All men are mortal'; accordingly he maintained that the formulation of a major premise is not a necessary condition to establish the conclusion that the Duke of Wellington is mortal. Mill's intention in his analysis of the syllogism is to show that the results of syllogistic reasoning can be obtained by reasoning from particulars to particulars, that the syllogism, although valid and of practical value, is logically superfluous.

Despite his perspicacity Mill did disservice to his theory by holding that the comparison of particular cases is always a form of induction. He was preoccupied with the methods of establishing propositions about matters of fact, and it is natural to suppose that in their verification the cases considered must be cases of actual fact, and the procedure adopted must involve inference from observed instances to those not yet observed. It is less apparent, though true, that the consideration of possible cases may also play a role. Mill overlooked the possibility that deliberative reasoning can lead to the solutions of factual problems, and that even when matters of fact are at issue, reflective reasoning by the direct comparison of instances is different from induction.

Wittgenstein remarked that justification comes to an end. There is what might be called an 'end' to justification, although the picture of reaching a terminus is misleading. Deliberative case by case procedures of justification are 'open ended', in the sense that for every reason given for saying 'This is K' it is *always possible* to give some other equally good or equally bad reason. There is an end to reasoning but no end of reasons; there is a point where no more cases need to be given, but there is no final, terminal case. Unless it is understood that this feature is not a *defect* in reasoning, there will be an irresistible temptation to ask, when cases of K and of not-K are mentioned in support of a case at issue to show it is K, how it is that those cases presented in support are themselves justified as being K or not-K; and this dissatisfaction may not be overcome by replying that further instances should be called up, for this will seem to be no answer. For, it will be said, it is always possible to ask of any case 'What justifies this as being K?', and since the question can be asked of any reply that presents only more cases, no such reply can meet it.

We are familiar with the child who asks 'Why?' of every reason given him. His persistent questioning shows more than exceptional curiosity, for it shows he has grasped something of the peculiar logical powers of the question he continues to put. We recognize that often his parents have given satisfactory answers to the child's initial queries; we may not notice that by continuing to ask 'Why?' he may be exercising his discovery of a kind of question different from those he has met before. He has discovered that, unlike 'Who is that man?' or 'What colour are these flowers?', this form of question is always logically in order. He has yet to discover that it is not always to the point. The situation is somewhat similar when the chronic request is for justification. A person may ask 'What justifies this as being of kind K?' and not be in the position of the child. On the other hand, a person may ask this question of *every* case of K and of not-K that has been, is, or will be put before him and think that the question has not been answered for no better reason than that it can still be asked intelligibly. His question is such that an answer to it in terms of particular cases is at once a request for the same form of question again. For example, suppose a man sees a chimney pot and asks what supports it. He is told it is supported by the chimney. But what supports the chimney? The stone foundations. What supports the foundations? The ground beneath. Now suppose he asks, 'What supports the ground?' He may think that unless *this* question is answered no right answer has been given to the question of how the chimney pot is supported. And this is absurd. He may think that so long as this type of question *can* be asked, no reply will be satisfactory. What he wants is not only a reply which will meet his question, but also a reply that will make it impossible for a question of this kind to be asked any further, and no such reply is forthcoming. He has not seen that the replies given to him have met his question; that his technique of questioning has gone beyond a point where the sought-for answer has been provided, and that now the procedure of questioning is followed for its own sake.

All this underlines the point that giving reasons for the application of a concept to a particular case is an inexhaustible process which may yet come to a decisive finish. If a person wants to justify that a particular case is one of a certain kind, it will do to have him compare that case with other cases of that kind and still others that are of other kinds. He will never come to the end of the possible comparisons he might make. But he may reach a stage where there is no need and no point in carrying out further comparisons, even though those comparisons could always be carried out, and even though those comparisons which he does not make are as relevant to his problem as those which he does make. Just as, for instance, a person who looks and listens to a bird for some time may have seen and heard enough to say what kind of bird it is and finds further looking and listening unrewarding, it may become *apparent* to one who carries out comparison after comparison that the case before him is one of a certain kind.

Of course one likely objection is that reasoning by the comparison of cases may convince a person of the truth of a statement but can do nothing to justify or conclusively show it is true, for reasoning of this kind is no more than 'psychological'. Well, let us say it is 'psychological', no harm is done; one might say this also of a deductive proof. If a person should suppose that because people sometimes accept an argument by instances when it is unsound, it follows that argument by instances can never be conclusive, he might as well suppose that because people sometimes accept invalid arguments it follows that no arguments are valid. To say that an argument is 'psychological' is simply to say that it is persuasive, perhaps calculated to win assent, and that it is convincing; and this makes no comment on whether the argument is sound or fallacious, or whether it fails or succeeds in being conclusive. A person who remarks by way of objection that argument by instances is 'psychological' claims more than merely that the argument is convincingly presented, for he has in mind also that there is some flaw in it, that it fails to establish the conclusion it seems to prove. These two claims are quite independent of one another, for it most certainly does not follow that an argument *is* unsound, inconclusive, contains hidden flaws, or is in some way dubious, simply from the fact that it is presented in a manner designed to convince people of its truth. To say that argument by instances is psychological *therefore* it is not conclusive argument, is a *non-sequitur*.

Philosophers in the past have given official recognition only to two forms of justificatory procedure, logical demonstrations and empirical inductions, and these have become identified with the concept of justification itself. Wisdom asks us to take a fresh look at the nature of the concept and to become aware of the procedure that ultimately gives one a right to judge that something is a thing of a certain sort. That procedure is one of referring to particular cases. Though a person may have justification for thinking that something is a thing of a certain sort without knowing the definition of things of that sort, or without having reasoned by deduction, he would have *no* justification for thinking that something is a thing of a certain sort without the consideration and comparison of instances of that sort and instances not of that sort.

5

Sceptical Doubts

1. *Foreword*

There is a pattern of reasoning common to sceptical theories about our knowledge of the material world. First, a person must ultimately rely on the data of his sensations as evidence for asserting any statement about the existence of material things, and he has no reason for asserting any such statement apart from his experience of these data; from them he infers conclusions about the material world. It will be held by a sceptic that the inference is neither inductive nor deductive and therefore any conclusion reached by its means is unjustified.

Alternatively it may be held (though not by a sceptic) that the inference, so far from being deductive, is in fact causal. Or again in opposition to a sceptic, it will be said that the inference is not inductive, and that statements about material things are logically reducible to statements about sensations and therefore can be verified on the grounds of sensory data: the inference is in this way formally valid.

The sceptic, the causal theorist and the phenomenalist conduct their manipulations safely within the precincts of the doctrine described in the first chapter. Most noticeably this appears in attempts to bridge a sceptic's gap either by a deductive or by a causal argument. It appears, of course, in a sceptic's claim that there *is* a gap because neither form of inference is possible.

If there is a problem about the connection between statements about the material world and statements about that which gives one a right to make them, there is also a problem about the connection between statements about sensations and that which gives one a right to make *them*. Surprisingly, philosophical reflection about the logic of the connection between the first two has led to doubt, while philosophical reflection about the logic of the connection between the second two has led to certainty. And the problem has become one of deciphering the connection between one class of propositions which for philosophical reasons seem doubtful, and another class of propositions which for philosophical reasons seem beyond doubt.

The basis for the judgement of doubt on the one hand, and of certainty on the other, in large-scale terms is this. The connection between the first two, above, is propositional, although the connection between the second two is not. Wherever there is a connection between propositions it can be asked whether it is necessary or contingent; and if it is neither there is a move to deny they are connected at all, and especially to deny that the one could be a reason for the other. But wherever there is no connection between proposition, the issue of the inductive or deductive credentials of their connection does not arise. Consequently if there is a connection but not a propositional connection, the standard criticism cannot be brought to bear. It is thought, therefore, that no criticism can be brought to bear.

2. *Scepticism about material things*

Sceptical paradoxes about material things mainly take two different forms of doubt. The first form of doubt is the outright denial that there are any material things at all: that chairs, tables, human bodies, or any other items which are material things, do not exist. The second, more moderate, form, of doubt does not deny that material things exist, or that there are material things such as chairs, tables and human bodies, but does deny that anyone can *know* that there are any material things. A philosopher who proposed a doubt of the first sort would not assert that he believed that there are material things, or that material things possibly exist, whereas a philosopher who proposed the second form of doubt might. He might say that he feels sure the coins in his pocket exist and are material objects, that it is absurd to doubt it; but that he cannot be absolutely certain that there are coins in his pocket and that neither he nor anyone else could know it. Obviously a philosopher may entertain the lesser doubt without the stronger one, although the converse is false: to say that there are no material things is to say also that no one can know, or be certain, that there are. The thoroughgoing and the moderate sceptics agree that statements about material things are made on the grounds of immediate sensory data which a person experiences, and the thoroughgoing sceptic may argue that nothing exists apart from the data which are experienced, while the moderate sceptic may argue that it is not known that anything exists apart from them.

It is easier to see what is denied by the more moderate doubt than by the uncompromising claim that there are no material things at all. Sometimes the expression 'There are no material things' is so used that there is no contradiction in saying, for example, 'Here are chairs and tables, but there are no material things'. In this case, what is meant by saying that there are no material things is also what is meant by saying that material things are nothing more than sensations; that the phrase 'Here are chairs and tables' is understood to be only a way of expressing some statement about sensations. No doubt this is what Berkeley intended by denying the existence of material bodies or substances, and whatever impression Berkeley may have conveyed he did not mean to assert that a person who says 'Here are chairs and tables' would always be speaking falsely. The form of words of a thoroughgoing sceptic in many cases simply serves to introduce a type of phenomenalism. Are there any philosophers, who by denying that material things exist, have *not* meant to assert a form of phenomenalism? Such a philosopher would be committed to holding that an expression like 'Here are chairs and tables' is always and in every case false and that there is *no* sense in which one might say chairs, or even human bodies, exist. Moore has said 'that *some* have *sometimes* meant this, is, I think certain' and he may have had McTaggart in mind.[1]

The proposal that no one can know for certain that there are material objects has been much more frequently entertained, if not as a conclusion then at least as a 'hypothesis' to be refuted. And it is *this* doubt rather than the outright denial that material things exist

[1] Moore, 'Reply to my Critics', *The Philosophy of G. E. Moore*, ed. P. A. Schilpp, New York 1942, p. 670; see Wisdom, 'Moore's Technique', ibid., p. 439.

Although McTaggart had said 'the result is that matter is in the same position as the Gorgons or the Harpies' here supporting Moore, he also said 'we sacrifice neither the experience of everyday life nor the results of science by denying the existence of matter. We only sacrifice a theory of metaphysics which we have already seen cannot be justified.' *Some Dogmas of Religion,* pp. 95-6.

which will be the main subject of our investigations. It doubts that there is any adequate way to *justify* saying that we ever know of material objects; or, as Stout remarked, 'It is not the claim of physical things to exist which is on trial, but only the claim of a certain theory to account for the way in which we know of their existence or are justified in believing them to exist.'[1] The traditional arguments supporting this doubt begin by pointing to difficulties which seem inextricably present in a common sense view of the world. It is common sense to suppose that while things sometimes are not as they appear, most of the time they are; that most objects have definite, fixed shapes and sizes which can be found out by examining then measuring them; that normally two persons looking at the same object will see the same thing; that a chair which a person saw a moment ago before turning away is the same chair he now sees by looking at it again; that a blue crayon *is* blue and does not merely seem blue to him. And it is of course a common sense belief that we all do know to be true enormous numbers of propositions about chairs and tables and human bodies, and about an indefinite number of other things. A sceptic alleges that there are serious and important defects in these beliefs. Let us look at the kind of cases used to support this claim.

The first group of instances concern illusions and hallucinations. Illusions are cited to show that on occasions something which *is* the case does not *appear* to be the case, or that what *appears* to be so is actually not so. The job of illusions is not to establish that what a person perceives is unreal, but only that he wrongly perceives something which is real. The examples are familiar, diverse and there is no end of them: a straight stick looks bent when thrust in water; the slope on a distant hillside appears flat; a tight hat feels as if it were on one's head even after it has been removed; a cloak hung up in the moonlight seems to a person to be the body of a friend; to a jaundiced man everything looks yellow; and so on.

The point of hallucinatory cases is somewhat different. They illustrate that on some occasions things which seem to exist in fact do not, or that things which a person takes or thinks to be real are quite unreal. The drunkard, the hypnotized man or the mescaline-taker see rats when there are no rats present; the feverish man hears voices when no

[1] *Mind and Matter*, p. 241.

one is speaking. Like illusions, the examples which philosophers have conceived of hallucinations are endless.

The second group of instances concern the diversity of observers and vantage points. Unlike examples of illusions and hallucinations, the relevant cases in this group are not in the first place aimed at showing that a person is deceived or deluded. Instead they are intended to show that physical objects look, appear or seem different to differently placed observers, or different to the same observer from different positions of observation. Some popular samples: A penny may look circular to one observer and elliptical to another, or look circular to one observer from one vantage point and elliptical when he changes his position; the shape of a table seems rectangular when viewed from above, elongated when viewed at the horizontal; the same water may feel warm to one person, cool to another, or warm to one person's right hand and cool to his left; the viewed shape of an envelope changes as it is waved about.

Both groups of examples are employed to create dilemmas concerning common beliefs by driving a logical wedge between statements about sensations and statements about physical objects. The cases mentioned are not, of course, all the cases which have been used, nor are the dilemmas which seem to follow the only ones there are. Yet the cases are typical and the dilemmas we will take up are representative. Two notorious examples propel the argument directly to dilemmas that lead to sceptical doubts:

a. A penny may seem circular to one person and at the same time elliptical to a second observer; if the penny really is circular, then it merely seems elliptical to one of the observers; if it really is elliptical then to the other observer it merely seems circular; but the penny cannot be both circular and elliptical at once, so one observer must not be perceiving the real shape of the penny. Further, there is reason to suppose that neither observer perceives the real penny since there are an infinite number of possible vantage points from which the penny could be observed, and so an infinite number of possible shapes which might be seen, any one of which might be *the* shape of the penny. How then are we to say what the penny really is like? Even if we grant that one observer may be perceiving the real shape of the penny, we should still never be certain which shape it is, since there is no more reason in favour of one observed shape than there is in favour of any of the others.

b. A second dilemma arises from cases of mistaken observation. If our observations are sometimes in error, what reasons have we to think that they are not always in error? We can of course correct a mistaken observation: we find on subsequent examination that the stick was not really bent, that the oasis was a mirage. But the data of correction are of the same sort as are the data corrected; still more experience might show that the stick was not straight after all, or that the oasis was not a mirage. It is only on the basis of further sense-experience that a person could certify the credentials of any observations he has already made; consequently he cannot establish, without begging the question, that his observations are in any instance really trustworthy.

Or again, although a person may be convinced that what he is holding is a book, it is at least possible that subsequent events will show him to have been wrong; it may turn out that, for example, he had been hypnotized at the time, or that he was dreaming at the time, and now has to withdraw his claim that he was holding a book. And obviously at any given time in his experience he is in the position of a person who might have reason, later on, to say that his experience was other than what he had been convinced it was.

No doubt these stock cases are contrived and artificial, and non-philosophical puzzlement about them is rare. Yet we must use caution in criticizing them along these lines. For one thing, the examples are (in a sense) too easy to discredit. A circular penny does not *look* elliptical when I am looking at it from an angle, say, when I see it on a shelf: it looks circular, the way a circular thing looks when seen from an angle. Nor does it *seem* or *appear* to have a peculiar, untypical shape at any point in its career simply because it is not always viewed straight on. No one thinks for a moment that the clock face in the shop window seems first elliptical, then circular, and finally elliptical again as he walks by gazing at it. This criticism is sound. But there is a danger in using it to *dismiss* the examples and the scepticism arising from them. For these points create the false impression that the mistake which a sceptic makes, indeed the reason for his scepticism, is now exposed: that his error is to misuse language in describing these cases. To point out this as an error does not explain *why* a sceptic introduces these specific examples and takes, as this criticism suggests, special license with them.

To return. The terminus of these representative dilemmas is a conclusion which provides the excuse for a variety of closely linked philosophical theories. They contend that a person can know and be certain that one special sort of thing, his own sensations, exist, without having to give any argument or proof; but he cannot know and be certain of the existence of any other sorts of things unless some proof can be given. And the acceptable proof is, as we expect, a demonstrative proof, or failing that, an inductive justification.

One of the best illustrations of this situation in epistemology comes from a passage in Russell's *Problems of Philosophy*. He combines the essential elements of the predicament: the common sense belief in material objects, the discrediting example, the certainty of one's own sensations and the ensuing philosophical puzzle.

One great reason why it is felt that we must secure a physical object in addition to the sense-data, is that we want the *same* object for different people. When ten people are sitting round a dinner-table, it seems preposterous to maintain that they are not seeing the same tablecloth, the same knives and forks and spoons and glasses. But the sense-data are private to each separate person; what is immediately present to the sight of one is not immediately present to the sight of another: they all see things from slightly different points of view, and therefore see them slightly differently. Thus, if there are to be public neutral objects, which can be in some sense known to many different people, there must be something over and above the private and particular sense-data which appear to various people. What reason, then, have we for believing that there are such public neutral objects?[1]

We may simplify the large-scale problem which Russell introduces. The ultimate evidence for asserting anything about material objects never consists itself of material objects, rather it consists of sensations of individual observers; accordingly any assertion about material

[1] Pp. 31–2.

objects is ultimately an *inference* from these sensations. The problem is to explain how an inference of this special sort can be justified, if it can be justified at all. Let us consider the outlines of four standard attempts to solve it.

i. 'The inference is causal' – This argument, a form of which is found in Locke, asserts that the inference from statements about sensations to statements about material objects is an inference from effect to cause. Holders of this theory allow that a person may causally infer conclusions about material things on the grounds of premises consisting of statements about sensations, since the sensations an observer experiences are caused by properties of the material object. As it stands, the theory is vulnerable to cases of illusions, hallucinations, relativity of perceptions and so on; because of these cases, if material things exist they must be different from the sense-experiences people have. Consequently philosophers have introduced a special theory of perception proposing, for example, that while an object may seem white to one observer and yellow to another at the same time, or look different to the same observer at different positions, the material object itself does not change in this way. What a person perceives is not the material object: rather, the real, material object is something other than the sense-impressions of colour, sound, taste, and touch which a person experiences, and these sense-impressions 'represent' the material object. This theory is a natural one to adopt in the light of cases of illusion and, especially, examples of the relativity of different perceptions; it is almost forced upon one, for instance, by the 'double image argument'. Moore says,

A serious objection seems to me to be that, when we see a thing double (have what is called a 'double image' of it), we certainly have *two* sense-data each of which is *of* the surface seen, and which cannot therefore both be identical with it; and that yet it seems as if, if any sense-datum is ever identical which the surface *of* which it is a sense-datum, each of these so-called 'images' must be so. It looks, therefore, as if every sense-datum is, after all, only 'representative' of the surface, *of* which it is a sense-datum.[1]

[1] *Philosophical Papers*, pp. 56–7.

Moore does not go on to hold that the image which an observer experiences is caused by properties of the material object which it is supposed to represent. But supposing this to be held, it seems possible to pass from sensations to material objects by means of a causal inference; if there is a tomato which I see then my sense-impression of that tomato is caused by properties in a material object called a tomato. The inference, however, has a striking feature: the cause, whose effects we experience as sense-impressions, is never perceived and never could be perceived. The peculiarity of the theory is that the inference is always one from an experienced effect to a cause of which no experience is possible.

ii. 'The inference cannot be causal' – Berkeley saw that the causal theory was a solution only at the price of an unjustifiable inference. His argument draws upon the contrast between two kinds of inference situations. A person who sees smoke and infers he will see the fire which causes it, if he goes and looks, can check up on his inference by going and looking: he infers further sensations from sensations he has already experienced. But if a person who sees a penny infers the existence of a material object as the cause of his sensations, there is no comparable way for him to check up on his inference; it is a tautology that any further sensations he may have of the penny will be further sensations, and it is logically impossible for him to perceive the material object he supposes must exist, for that object could not be perceived and could not have been perceived. The only procedure available to him to verify the result of his inference to a material object is a procedure which by its very nature could not succeed. Since the claim that material things exist as a cause of sensations could be established only by means of the experience of sensations, and since material things cannot be perceived, the claim could not be established at all. A philosopher who accepts the representative theory, the criticism runs, is like a painter who does a portrait and says it is a good likeness of the subject, but when asked to *show* it is a good likeness produces a second portrait as proof of the resemblance.

Variations of the attack occur in a variety of forms with the intention of discrediting the thesis that the existence of material objects can be inductively inferred from data consisting wholly of immediate sense-experiences. If physical objects are to be verified, Russell argues, they must have some kind of correlation with sense-data, and must be verifiable through their correlation *alone*.

But how is the correlation itself ascertained? A correlation can only be ascertained empirically by the correlated objects being constantly *found* together. But in our case, only one term of the correlation, namely, the sensible term, is ever *found* . . . Therefore, it would seem, the correlation with objects of sense . . . is itself utterly and forever unverifiable.[1]

The argument exposes the theory, not as proceeding from instances which have been observed to those which have not yet been observed, but rather from those which have been immediately perceived to those which could not have been and could not be immediately perceived. It contends that if the existence of material objects can be inferred from sensations the inference cannot be verified empirically.

iii. 'The inference is deductive' – This explanation proposes that to any statement about a material thing there corresponds an equivalent set of statements of indefinite length referring only to sensations. It is possible to reduce a statement about a material thing to sets of statements descriptive of sensations somewhat in the way in which a statement about the age of the average London schoolboy can be logically reduced to sets of statements descriptive of the ages of individual London schoolboys. To assert 'There is a tomato in the basket' is simply to assert no more and no less than some number of statements about immediate sense-experiences; and since any statement about a material thing is equivalent to some sets of statements about sensations, the inference from the one to the other is deductive. This phenomenalist position is a reformulation of Berkeley's alternative to Locke's theory, for Berkeley represents an assertion about the existence of material objects as merely a way of asserting something about immediate sense-experiences: to assert that there is a tomato in the basket is to assert what might equally have been expressed in terms of statements about ideas, about sense-impressions. By proposing that statements about material things are logically reducible to statements about sensations, the original problem of explaining the relationship between them appears to have been solved.

[1] *Mysticism and Logic*, London 1917, pp. 145–6.

iv. 'The inference cannot be deductive' – In opposition to the phenomenalist explanation are two arguments designed to show that on no
occasion is a statement M about material things logically reducible to
statements $S_1 \ldots S_n$ about sensations. For it may be argued by a
sceptic that while an infinite number of statements descriptive of sensations would be equivalent to a statement of sort M, we never have
and never could have that number of statements. Alternatively it may
be argued that even an infinite number of statements descriptive of
sensations could not be equivalent to a conclusion of sort M, for it is
logically possible to assert that statements $S_1 \ldots S_n$ are true, that these
statements exhaust the evidence we have for asserting M, and also
assert that M is false, that the contradictory of M is logically compatible
with the assertion of any statements descriptive of sensations from
which M is derived. From either of these arguments a sceptic may conclude that statements about material things which we do not know
immediately are not logical consequences of statements about sensations which we do know immediately: accordingly statements about
material things are not logically equivalent to, or reducible to, statements about sensations.

This argument returns the issue to the original question of whether,
or how, knowledge of statements about the material world is justified.
If we cannot justify our beliefs about the existence of material things
either by inductive or deductive inference from the data of sensations
then it is not at least possible that any or all of these beliefs are mistaken? It begins to seem as if a sceptic is correct after all. But this seems
preposterous in the light of Moore's arguments that we *do* sometimes
know for certain such things as the 'Here is a hand'. The problem is to
reconcile this apparently irreconcilable situation.

In these attempts to explain the connections between the conclusions
to be justified and the reasons that justify them, there is a confusion
whether the problem under investigation concerns empirical or non-
empirical issues. Berkeley seems to be proposing an hypothesis to
rival Locke's about the sort of things which as a matter of fact exist.
A sceptic seems to be claiming that we have in fact no knowledge of a
certain kind of things, material objects, although we do have knowledge of a certain other kind of things, sense-data. What is in question
is sometimes the *cause* of sensations which are themselves *effects*; it is

G

questioned whether certain entities *exist* or whether anyone does know
they exist. The arguments seem to be attempts to ascertain the *sort of
things* a person is aware of when he perceives something. Nevertheless the success or failure of these arguments seems to turn, not on
questions of fact, but on questions of logic; that a physical object, a
penny, cannot both be elliptical and circular at the same time; that a
person cannot empirically verify a cause which cannot be perceived;
that statements about material objects differ in verification from statements about sense-data, or that no amount of sense-data reports are
adequate to infer validly the existence of a material object. The arguments proceed as if they were *a priori*, the issues at stake seem empirical.
This two-sided treatment of problems about the external world, in
which psychology is mixed with logic and questions of fact are confused with purely reflective questions, is a predominate characteristic
of the epistemology of Locke, Berkeley and Hume. It is present also
in Moore, where we sometimes find a wavering conception of the
nature of the problems at issue.

Even though Moore has represented himself to be concerned with
the analysis of propositions, he has frequently represented himself as
in ignorance of what is in fact the case, for he has asked such questions as,

> *What*, when I know '*This* is *part of the surface of* a human hand',
> am I knowing about the sense-datum in question? Am I, in this case,
> really knowing about the sense-datum in question that it *itself* is
> part of the surface of the human hand?
> Can we hold that this sense-datum really is identical with this part
> of the surface of this inkstand?[1]

On occasions Moore represents himself as like a man who is not sure
whether what he sees is part of a sofa or a piece of cloth pinned on to
it, or like a man who is not sure whether what he sees is an after-image
or a patch on the wall. On other occasions he represents himself as like
a man who is not sure he has got the right answer to whether a certain
conclusion about the average man is an accurate expression of statements about individual men, or like a statistician doubtful about the
results of his analysis. He is drawn between representing himself, on

[1] *Philosophical Papers*, p. 55; *Philosophical Studies*, London 1922, p. 239.

the one hand, as concerned with matters of fact, and on the other, as concerned with the *a priori* relations between statements; between, on the one hand, questions about the contingent relations between a person's sense-data and the surface of a material thing, and on the other, reflective questions about the logical relations between propositions referring to sense-data and propositions referring to material things. It is often unclear which he has in mind, or that he does not mean to be concerned with both.

We should be struck by the philosophical tendency, not found only in Moore, to present the problem first in one way as a contingent problem and then in another way as a problem of analysis. This is precisely the same unstable combination of fact and logic implicit in the traditional causal and phenomenalist theories of perception, and implicit in scepticism; for a sceptic derives what appear to be empirical conclusions, factual doubts, from reasons which are completely *a priori*. Until it is plain how and why scepticism is divorced from nature it will be obscure what it is that scepticism expounds.

3. *A sceptic's hypotheses*

In philosophy it seems not uncommon for two rival hypotheses to be both able to account for all the facts. Thus, for example, it is possible that life is one long dream, and that the outer world has only that degree of reality that the objects of dreams have.[1]

This is a typical sceptical doubt expressed in the form of a factual assertion; rivalling, apparently, the firm conviction which people have, and which seems absurd to call an hypothesis, that the world and real life is not a dream-world or dream-life.

Before examining its peculiarities, it is worth taking a second look at the general behaviour of sceptical doubts. If sceptical doubts were doubts about matters of fact then they could be confirmed or discredited by appealing at some stage to empirical data; but a striking feature of them is that they cannot gain or lose their credentials in this way. Characteristically, the procedure by which a sceptic supports his doubt is a completely non-empirical one and different from any scientific procedure; he does not attempt to test his 'hypothesis' in the light

[1] Russell, *Problems of Philosophy*, p. 191.

of empirical facts, but proceeds to establish its truth wholly by *argument*. In the course of this argument his denial that material objects can be known becomes transformed into a doubt about the reasons, justification and proof for saying they can be known. This by itself is insufficient to show that a sceptic's argument is *a priori*, for a person may deny a statement of fact and explain his denial by saying that there are, in fact, no reasons for asserting the statement. But a sceptic does more than this, for he claims that *any* reasons which could *conceivably* be given would fail to show that material objects are known to exist. He is concerned with the reasoning used in support of all statements of a given kind and not merely with the reasoning supporting some, though not other, statements of that kind. And he does not allow the possibility that his scepticism might, in the light of *any* empirical facts, be shown to be wrong. It is a correct assessment of a sceptic's arguments that no amount of empirical investigation could change his views: he is asserting that material things could not possibly be known and not merely that they are not as a matter of fact known.

But let us suppose that the conjecture that all of a person's experience takes place in a dream *is* a factual hypothesis; it is therefore appropriate to take empirical measures to ascertain its truth or falsehood and some empirical facts could count for or against it. Yet none do.

If someone said to me 'You may be dreaming right now', as I sit at my desk, it is certain I could show that he is mistaken; and although the assertion 'I am not dreaming right now' is an obscure remark on its own, it is proper to reply, 'But I am *not* dreaming'.

The first case to consider is one in which I am certain that I am awake, conscious, and not dreaming. I am sitting at my desk; and there is a very simple empirical test which will show me, and anyone watching, that I am awake and not asleep and dreaming; I simply push back my chair and say 'Look – I am awake'; or I get up from my chair, walk across the room, fetch a book and read aloud from it. There are innumerable things of a very similar sort which could be done and which would show that I am awake and not dreaming.

The second case to consider is one which sometimes though infrequently happens, when a person who is awake and not dreaming is suddenly struck by the thought that he may not be awake and that he may actually be dreaming. Of course he is quite wrong in his momentary supposition, nevertheless he does for a moment doubt that he is awake. It is possible for me to wake up in a strange place and in surroundings I fail to recognize and think momentarily that I am dreaming; if, for example, I woke up in an unfamiliar hotel room and thought I was actually dreaming when in fact I was observing the unaccustomed surroundings, I might then suddenly be under a misapprehension about whether I was dreaming or not. And one decisive way in which I could settle the matter would be to get up out of bed. This or some other very similar act could correct my misapprehension that I was not awake at the time. There are of course cases where people have wakened in hospital, not knowing how they got there, and in their confusion really have doubted for some moments whether they were conscious and that their surroundings were real: they *have* thought they were dreaming when they were not, and obviously there are endless numbers of ways in which it might be shown to them that they are not dreaming.

In cases of each of these two kinds, if I had some reason to think 'But I must be dreaming all this', I could at least pinch myself soundly, and that would be quite an adequate self-imposed test of whether I was dreaming at the time. It is plain that we do distinguish empirically between dreaming and waking in countless ways, and that in spite of the constant intermittent states of sleeping and waking which everyone of us undergoes, there is in fact almost never any difficulty in distinguishing between them.

Now everything said in the last few paragraphs is completely beside the point if it is intended to *refute* the sceptical conjecture that the whole outer world may be nothing but a dream. For Russell could reply that everything that can be done in waking life, including the tests which have been mentioned, could also be done in a dream. A person could dream he is dreaming or that he is waking up, that he is pinching himself or that he is philosophizing about dreaming. It is important to notice that a sceptic need not listen to cases of the sort just mentioned: he has an *a priori* formula which can always be employed, by asking how one knows that the test of his being awake is not itself something which is dreamt. He can dismiss in advance every piece of empirical evidence which would normally be accepted as showing whether a person is asleep or awake, dreaming or not; yet he *knows* there is overwhelming empirical evidence to show that there are some occasions on which people are dreaming and others on which they are not. The fact that Russell does not admit any evidence of this kind as a *possible* refutation makes it clear that his 'hypothesis' is immune to the possibility of empirical disproof and is not a contingent proposition. It is not an hypothesis at all. Russell's conjecture comes to adding after every statement about waking life, 'but it could be a dream'. How is this conjecture to be explained?

A sceptic will argue that although we believe there is a difference between dreaming and waking life this difference cannot be conclusively established. He will hold that it is impossible to tell with certainty which is the prevailing state at any time and that in consequence, as Russell says, it may be that the whole of life is a dream. What are the arguments which might be given for holding this? It seems that Russell gives two arguments although it is not immediately plain which is the one from which he thinks it follows that the whole of life may be a dream. Let us take them separately.

i. He says 'There is no logical impossibility in the supposition that the whole of life is a dream, in which we ourselves create all the objects that come before us. But although this is not logically impossible, there is no reason whatever to suppose that it is true.'[1] Now in this passage Russell might be understood to mean merely that it is logically possible that my present sense-experiences might have been dream experiences, even if they are not, and that the proposition 'I am not now dreaming' or 'The whole of life is not a dream' is contingent and not logically true. But this would not entail the propositions which Russell wants to establish, namely that my present sense-experiences *may* really be dream-experiences or that the whole of life *may* be a dream. There is no contradiction in asserting 'I know for certain that my present sense-experiences are not merely dream-experiences, although they might have been dream-experiences'. From the fact that proposition P is contingent it does not follow that P *may* be false, although it would follow, if P were true, that P *might have been* false, and if P were false, that P *might have been* true; and if Russell's point were that, since P is a contingent proposition, namely 'The whole of life is not a dream', P may be false, he would not have established his conclusion. Further,

---

[1] *The Problems of Philosophy*, p. 35.

if Russell means merely that the proposition 'The whole of life is not a dream' is doubtful since it is a contingent proposition and not a logically true proposition, this is difficult to reconcile with his belief that there are other propositions, such as 'It seems to me as if I were not dreaming', which he allows can be known to be true by the speaker and which are also contingent. He must not mean merely that a proposition is doubtful so long as it is not necessarily true. By saying that there is no logical impossibility in the supposition that the whole of life is a dream, Russell must mean something else.

ii. He must mean, instead, that it is logically possible that my present experiences consist in dream-experiences which very closely resemble sense-experiences I should be having if I were awake, and which are the data I have for believing that I am awake; and that because all the data which I have for my belief that I am awake and not dreaming leave it possible that my belief is false, it may be that my present experiences are dream-experiences. Russell must mean that the supposition that the whole of life may be a dream is logically compatible with a statement of the immediate experiences which a person might have as evidence for asserting its contradictory. For he says that the conjecture that the whole of life may be a dream 'is an uncomfortable possibility; but although it cannot be strictly *proved* to be false, there is not the slightest reason to suppose it is true', and in *An Outline of Philosophy* this same argument is given: 'It is impossible to prove, by a demonstrative argument, that we are not always dreaming; the best we can hope is a proof that this is improbable'.[1] In both these passages Russell gives the second but not the first of the two arguments mentioned. He holds that the immediately given data on which the propositions 'I am not now dreaming', 'All of us are not now dreaming' or 'The whole outer world is not a dream' are ultimately based are not data of the sort from which these propositions can be deduced. For example, Russell has argued elsewhere, 'I do not believe that I am now dreaming, but I cannot prove that I am not. I am, however, quite certain that I am having certain experiences, whether they be those of a dream or those of waking life'.[2] The experiences of which he is certain, he says, are those which he knows without making any inferences, his immediate sense-experiences which constitute the

[1] London 1927, p. 157.　　　[2] *Human Knowledge*, p. 186.

evidence he has both for his belief that he is dreaming or for his belief that he is not. Each belief is an inference from his immediate sensations and Russell's point is that although these beliefs are logically incompatible with one another, neither is logically incompatible with the immediate sense-experiences of which he is certain, and consequently the inference he makes is not deductive. For he goes on to describe an occasion on which he dreamt of seeing a church: 'It follows', he says, 'that the experience which I call "seeing a church" is not conclusive evidence that there is a church, since it may occur when there is no such external object as I suppose in my dream.' Russell must be holding, in this passage, that a statement descriptive of the immediate data which justify his belief that he is seeing a church is not logically incompatible with the statement that he only dreamt he was seeing a church. It is this argument, not the first one, which is adduced to establish that the whole of life may be a dream.

The strategy adopted by Russell is typical of philosophical scepticism about the physical world. The intention is to show that a person cannot prove, from the data of his sensations, that his experiences are those of external, physical objects, and not merely hallucinatory, illusory or dream experiences, for the reason that this conclusion cannot be derived by deduction or by induction from the grounds for asserting it. It is plain therefore that Russell's argument is not based on *facts* about dreaming. A sceptic reaches his paradoxical doubts by concentrating on the verificational logic of classes of propositions while neglecting the best evidence of observation.

4. *The search for certainty*

Oddly enough, one of the highways to scepticism is the belief that a philosophical investigation is a search for indubitable knowledge. The quest is seen as an attempt to justify philosophically that at any rate some contingent propositions are beyond doubt. By asking whether there is 'any knowledge in the world so certain that no reasonable man could doubt it' Russell introduces a pattern of reasoning that can be called the argument to incorrigibility. In its initial stages it covers familiar ground:

Let us take first the belief in common objects, such as tables and chairs and trees. We all feel quite sure about these in ordinary life, and yet our reasons for confidence are really very inadequate.

The argument characteristically attacks the reasons for a belief while admitting that the belief itself, that there are tables and chairs and that we know them, is not ordinarily doubted. Cases of illusion, hallucination and so on are used to establish a philosophical doubt:

> Naïve common sense supposes that they are what they appear to be, but that is impossible, since they do not appear exactly alike to any two simultaneous observers . . . If we are going to admit that the object is not what we see, we can no longer feel the same assurance that there is an object; this is the first intrusion of doubt.[1]

It is important to notice that the evidence given in support of this sort of doubt consists of an example which contrasts sensations with material objects, e.g.:

> And what we see is constantly changing in shape as we move about the room; so that here again the senses seem not to give us the truth about the table itself, but only about the appearance of the table.[2]

But if statements about the table are doubtful, there are, according to this argument, some things which can be known with certainty, namely a person's sense-data: about the existence of these a person cannot be

[1] *An Outline of Philosophy*, pp. 3-4.
[2] *Problems of Philosophy*, pp. 15-16.
Of course the example itself is faulty. The table a person sees is not changing its shape, like a cloud of smoke or an inflating balloon. If someone walks away and stands at a distance we do not think he has changed his shape and is now much smaller than he was before. If he *has* changed his shape it would make sense to measure this change. Perhaps Russell does not mean that the dimensions of an object are constantly changing but that it always *looks* as if they were. This is equally unsatisfactory: the person in the distance does not look five inches high, he looks as though he were of the same height but in the distance; as a man walks away from us he does not appear to be shrinking. 'Change in perspective' is not 'Change in shape', nor always change in appearance. Nevertheless, as mentioned before, emphasis on this kind of (completely fair) criticism can conceal the point behind the introduction of these examples, namely as a way of contrasting the verificational peculiarities of statements about sensations and statements about material objects.

wrong. Of the many versions of the argument to incorrigibility Price's is perhaps the most concise:

> When I see a tomato there is much that I can doubt. I can doubt whether it is a tomato that I am seeing, and not a cleverly painted piece of wax. I can doubt whether there is any material thing there at all. Perhaps what I took for a tomato was really a reflection; perhaps I am even the victim of some hallucination. One thing however I cannot doubt: that there exists a red patch of a round and somewhat bulgy shape, standing out from a background of other colour-patches, and having a certain visual depth, and that this whole field of colour is directly present to my consciousness.[1]

We may wonder at the eccentricity of Price's doubt for it is not, even remotely, connected with an ordinary doubt, say, whether fruit in a basket in a window is wax, or real, or perhaps just painted on a card. The very words Price uses disguise, to an extent, this eccentricity ('Perhaps what I took for a tomato was a reflection . . . an hallucination'). Perhaps in an ordinary, non-philosophical situation one is fooled by a reflection; and in an ordinary situation there is a standard way of finding out, by investigating to see whether it is a reflection, or what it is. Yet no investigation of this kind has an effect on Price's 'doubt'. In spite of the fact that, let us suppose, every shred of evidence confirms it is a real, physical, tomato, Price wishes to say that one *still* can doubt that it is a real, physical, tomato. Once again, nothing that would settle an ordinary doubt could settle this philosophical doubt. For in this oblique fashion Price is stating that when one says 'I see a tomato' one is not logically committed to assert that a material tomato exists, or, in his words, that 'there is any material thing there at all'.

Ordinarily, to say 'I see a tomato' is to leave oneself open to refutation if it happens that there is no tomato to be seen, and to accept the reply 'You don't see a tomato, there isn't one' as final if the apodosis is true. In this case one who says he *sees* a tomato would be as mistaken as if he had said, instead, 'There *is* a tomato'. But this is not the case that Price holds up. He has in mind a case in which a person who says 'I see a tomato' can be right even though no tomato exists. And these cases do occur, for instance, at the oculist's or in the psychological

[1] H. H. Price, *Perception*, 2nd edition, London 1950, p. 3.

laboratory. They have the feature of carrying a different implication from cases of the first kind, such that the statement 'I see a tomato' does not imply that a physical, material tomato exists. Part of the trouble here is that Price's example is too far removed from the precincts in which these unusual cases usually operate. In this passage the logic of the extraordinary case is allowed to become the logic of the ordinary case. Once this is done, it is a short step to link 'I can doubt Q' with 'Q is not a logical consequence of anything I cannot doubt'. The excuse which Price has for 'doubting' is not, as in a normal doubt, some suspicion that the tomato is artificial, or a reflection, but the fact that his statement that a tomato exists is not *entailed* by the reason he has for making it. Thus, one of his arguments comes to this: the fact that P does not entail Q gives a person a right to regard Q as doubtful when P is a statement describing one's immediate sensations and Q is not; that, for instance, 'There is a tomato' does not follow logically from the proposition 'There exists a red patch of round and somewhat bulgy shape etc . . . directly present to my consciousness', and so it can be doubted 'whether there is any material thing there at all'. But if Price's doubt arises from the traditional reason that there is no necessary connection present, his belief that he *cannot* doubt a proposition about his immediate consciousness has a different source.

Sometimes it is said that propositions of this kind can be known by a person 'without inference' and so differ from propositions about material objects which are known 'by inference'; and being known without inference they are known 'directly' – there is no interposing step which might be contested on the strength of its being neither causal nor necessary. The case for saying a person has 'incorrigible knowledge' of his own sensations rests upon the unique relationship between the grounds, the sensations he experiences, and his knowledge that a statement about his sensations is true. What gives a person the right to remark 'I am conscious of something red' is a particular sensation which he experiences, and this is, one might say, the ground or basis of his assertion. Given that particular sensation and a knowledge of the language, he knows that when he says 'I am conscious of something red' he is right, that his statement is true. But the sensation which gives him a right to assert this statement is not itself something which he *knows*, rather it is something he experiences, 'has' or 'is conscious of'. The ground or basis for his assertion is not known by him, but is experienced, and his statement is nothing he could be said to 'experience' or 'have', but is what he knows to be true. The relation between the statement and its basis is not one that could be questioned in the way in which a relation between propositions could be questioned. It is thought, therefore, that it could not be questioned. We have a rich and ready-made language for bringing out relations between one proposition and another, but none for registering the peculiarity of not-altogether-propositional connections like this. Calling a person's knowledge of his sensations 'incorrigible' is a way of indicating this special connection, and its difference from that propositional relationship which obtains when a person knows that a conclusion is true because it follows by deduction (or by induction) from premises which he knows to be true. When a philosopher says philosophically that he *cannot doubt* he signals platitudinously the oddity of the connection between his immediate sensations and a statement about them. When he says philosophically that he *can doubt* he signals paradoxically the oddity of the connection between a statement about his immediate sensations and a statement about the material world.

If we take the ascription of incorrigibility as signalling this special relationship, is it a mistake to say that a person's knowledge of his own sensations can be incorrigible? It is misleading, for it suggests that the prefixes 'I know for certain that . . .' 'I cannot doubt that . . .' when applied to a statement a person makes about his own sensations have a role over and above the role of the statement which they prefix. But it is not wrong. Of course, a speaker's knowledge is not incorrigible in the way in which his knowledge, say, of a necessarily true proposition is, or might be said to be, incorrigible. If one knows the meaning of the statement 'Things equal to the same thing are equal to each other' then he knows whether it is true regardless of who asserts it. But if one knows the meaning of 'I have a slight chill' he may not know whether it is true when it is asserted by someone else. To return then. Why does the prefix 'I know for certain' add nothing to the assertion (to continue Price's case) 'I am conscious of something red'?

If a man has a sensation of a certain sort that gives him a right to say he is conscious of something red, then if he says this he is right, and if he understands what he has said he knows that he is right. But there is an idiosyncratic feature of this situation: it does not allow for the possibility of his *not* knowing that what he says is correct, given the grounds for saying it and providing he understands what he says. If a person knows what 'I have a chill' means and says 'I have a chill' when he has a chill, he knows that what he says is true. Contrast this situation with a different one. A man may say 'I know that's a tomato in the basket' on the grounds of experiencing certain sensations; but given these grounds he might *not* have known it, and given these grounds what he says might *not* have been correct. If one knows what 'That's a tomato' means and says this on the grounds of seeing what seems to him to be a tomato, he might not know that what he says is true. In *this* case, by adding 'I know' a man is being informative about himself as well as about the existence of a tomato, for in addition to expressing the fact that there is a tomato, he is conveying that he knows this, something which he might not have known given these grounds. But in the previous case, be adding 'I know' a man is not being any more informative about himself than had he said merely that he *is* conscious of something red, for he is not expressing anything which might not have been so given his experiences and his understanding of his words. He is not, by adding 'I know for certain' to his assertion 'I am conscious of something red' expressing any additional information about his position in the way in which a man who adds 'I know for certain' to the statement 'That is a tomato in the basket' does. Even so, it is not a mistake to speak of a person as knowing that he is conscious of something, or is in pain; just as a person who says 'I feel pain' may know that what he says is false (e.g. when he does not feel pain), it is possible for him to know (when he does feel pain) that what he says is true. But if it is not wrong to say that a man knows for certain his own sensations, it is superfluous; for he conveys no more and no less than that he *is* experiencing a sensation. Price's claim 'I cannot doubt that I am conscious of something red' claims no more than 'I am conscious of something red', since given the grounds for saying the latter, a man who says and understands this could not but know he is right: 'I know I have a reddish sensation' means merely that I *have* one, and say I have.[1] A person who says 'I know I feel a chill', unlike one who

[1] See John Wisdom, *Other Minds*, VII, Oxford 1965; Wittgenstein, *Philosophical Investigations*, 276.

says 'I know I am shivering', has in his statement stated the reasons for his knowledge.

One difficulty about phrases like 'I know I feel a chill . . . am in pain, etc.' is not that they are incorrect, but that they *suggest* what is incorrect, for they suggest that *only* in such cases can a person have knowledge of a contingent statement. But nothing is gained by 'I know I feel a chill' not already expressed by 'I feel a chill', unless (possibly) *I know* is uttered for emphasis, like raising one's voice. To say of another person 'You don't know you feel a chill' is unintelligible unless it means 'You don't feel a chill'; the prefix 'You don't know' is redundant but not wrong. The role of the expression 'I know' changes when prefixing statements like 'That's a tomato'; to say 'I know' here stakes a claim which is not absurd to challenge by saying 'You don't know'; to say 'I know that's a tomato' is not only to claim it is certain that's a tomato but also that I know it; yet it may be certain without my knowing it, hence by saying 'I know' I convey something about my position as well as quite a different fact. This sharply contrasts with my statements about my sensations, for if I assert and understand the words 'I know I feel a chill' it cannot be certain that I feel a chill without my knowing these words express what is true. By contrasting the alleged incorrigibility of knowledge about one's own sensations with the corrigibility of knowledge about material things, a philosopher is not contrasting a type of statement which can be known with a type of statement which cannot. He is contrasting two different kinds of statements each of which can be known, and emphasizing that a man could not be wrong in asserting 'I am conscious of something red' in all of the ways in which he could be wrong in asserting 'There is a tomato in that basket'.

6

Scepticism and Necessity

1. *Foreword*

Berkeley is credited as having believed that if Locke were wrong he, Berkeley, must be right: that the alternative to the scepticism implicit in the *Essay* is the phenomenalism expounded in the *Principles*. Doubtless Berkeley misjudged the situation, but the satisfactory alternative is not the simple one that neither platform will do. It is the peculiar merit of phenomenalism in being wrong that the point at which it fails is precisely the point where scepticism necessarily succeeds. This is not to resurrect a sceptic's doubts, for the meaning of this central point in no way supports them. On the contrary, it shows they are groundless.

Part of the intention of this chapter is to show that the difference between statements about sensations and statements about physical objects which prevents the success of phenomenalism is one of the features which lies at the bottom of scepticism about the physical world. A sceptic claims that there is no demonstrable connection between what one says about the mental world and what one says about the material world. A phenomenalist claims that there *is* a demonstrable connection between what one says about both worlds, so to say something about the one is to say something about the other. Now there is a double difficulty here. First, neither party grasps that his efforts are directed towards providing an account or an explanation of the necessary differences between the types of statement at issue, and that when this is done no more need be done. In short, neither philosopher grasps the nature of his own philosophical exercise. Failing to see this, secondly, both a sceptic and a phenomenalist conduct their exercises under the misapprehension that whether or not knowledge of the material world is possible depends on which of the two theses comes out on top. They share the belief that if the problem cannot be solved by a deductive step, it cannot be solved at all. Accordingly the one strives to dismantle the equations the other strives to erect.

Scepticism is true, necessarily true, but not a menace. Phenomenalism is false, necessarily false, and a menace when thought to be true. For it conceals the truth in the scepticism it opposes, and only when the meaning of scepticism is recognized does it become plain that a sceptic's doubts are no reason for concern. Everyone knows that he knows what a sceptic says he cannot know, and a sceptic's arguments do nothing to show this to be false.

2. *Phenomenalism*

The variety of doctrines going under the name of phenomenalism can be separated, roughly, into those ostensibly about the facts of perception, at face-value theories about the actual constitution of the world, and explicit *a priori* accounts of the connections between classes of statements. Berkeley and Ayer illustrate the division, and it is the latter theory with which we will be chiefly concerned.

The thesis that statements about material objects are logically translatable into statements about sense-data is designed to provide a way of resolving the problems raised by a sceptic, by showing how it is possible that statements about material objects can be verified on the grounds of immediate sense-experiences. It is not a theory attempting to disclose which propositions about sensations or material things are true and which are false, but a meta-theory purporting to explain how their truth or falsehood is ascertained. It asserts that to any proposition M about material things there corresponds an equivalent proposition S about sensations, that a statement about a material thing is nothing more than a statement, or set of statements, about sensations; since the items of one's immediate experience consist only of sensations, propositions about material objects must be translatable without remainder into propositions about sensations. The doctrine (as it is often put) is that some such prefix as 'It *seems* to me now as if ....' signals a proposition whose reference is the immediate experiences of an observer, whereas the prefix 'It *is* the case that ...' introduces a proposition which can be translated deductively into sets of statements each prefixed in the former manner or by a hypothetical statement about what indivi-

dual observers would immediately experience. The proposed translation is a deductive step from how things *are* to how they *seem* to most
observers.

Among the translations of phenomenalism some are serious and
some are not. No one would hold, for instance, that its being cold in
London is a shorthand way of expressing the fact that to *Jones* it feels
cold in London, or an alternative way of stating that *everyone* in London
feels cold. The difficult case is not the purported reduction of statements
about the external world to statements about the sensations of a single
person, or of everyone; but where the reduction to a statement about
the sensations of most, or an indefinite number, of actual or potential
observers is attempted.

There is a flaw in this equivalence as well. Suppose the statement to
be verified is that there is a tiger in a cage at the zoo. If a person
denies that to most observers present and to most who might be
present it seems or would seem as if a tiger were in the cage – indeed if
he denies *every* statement about sensations in favour of concluding that
there is a tiger in the cage – and yet asserts that a tiger *is* in the cage, he
does not contradict himself. If he is right in his denial it does not follow
logically that his assertion about the presence of a tiger is false; it follows only that there is no reason to suppose that his assertion is true.
The proposition 'There is no reason for saying that p is true, yet p is
true' is irrational but not self-contradictory.

When the question is 'Does it seem to X as if there were a tiger in
the cage?' more importance is given to what X says of his sensations
than to the replies of others, for sensations as of a tiger give X a better
reason to answer the question than do sensations of a similar sort give
to anyone else. But when the question is 'Does it seem to most people
as if there were a tiger in the cage?' or 'Is there a tiger in the cage?' this
is not true. Yet there is still a difference between the latter expressions.
When the question is 'Does it seem to most people as if there were a
tiger in the cage?' more importance is given by X to what most people
say of their sensations than when the question is 'Is there a tiger in the
cage?'. The balance of the reasons that weigh with a person for answering the one question is different from the balance of the reasons that
weigh with him for answering the other. A person waiting on a crowd-
ed railway platform when asked 'Does the crowd think the train is

H

coming?' gives more attention, more weight, to his observation of the crowd picking up bags, collecting themselves to board a train and to murmurs of 'It's coming' than to the fact that he does, or does not, hear the train himself. But when asked 'Is the train coming?' he does not give that attention to his observations of the anticipatory behaviour of the crowd which he gives to his hearing the sound of the train, although he gives attention to both. Phenomenalist translations seem plausible because, both in the case of questions about what *is* so and in the case of questions about what to most observers *seems* so, a person includes among his reasons for answering his sensations of the behaviour and performances of other people, as well as his sensations of the situation in question. But this plausibility disappears with the recognition that the regard which a person gives to these different sets of sensations is different depending upon *which* question he is attempting to answer, and that the questions cannot be the same.

Philosophers have viewed phenomenalist programmes with increasing suspicion, no doubt partly because of the failure of phenomenalists to deliver the goods in the form of working translations. But doubts go deeper than this. It is often argued that the statement descriptive of sensations would itself be infinitely incomplete: there is no statement both necessary and sufficient to express the content of a statement about material things. Moreover, an analytic translation is prevented by the logical independence of the two types of statement: if the statement 'There is a tiger in the cage' is equivalent to, or means the same as, 'It seems or would seem to most observers as if there were a tiger in the cage', then to assert the first and deny the second, or assert the second and deny the first, would result in a contradiction. Yet no contradiction occurs. These well-known moves against phenomenalism would not read strangely to a sceptic, indeed they are an integral part of his attack against the views of common sense; these plausible arguments *against* phenomenalism are all arguments *for* scepticism.

If an equivalence cannot be sustained, and if there is no necessary connection between the two kinds of statement, does this mean that there is no connection between them? The remaining alternative, which it was the aim of phenomenalism to avoid, appears to be that the connection, if there is one, must be causal or contingent. This alternative has been rightly condemned and the arguments from Berkeley to

Russell need not be revived. The interesting question is whether, granting the failure of the causal theory, any connection between them could survive.

Phenomenalist theories derive partly from the apparent need to put down the conclusions of a philosophical sceptic. But there is another, perhaps more fundamental, motive. This is the conviction that if sensations are *reasons* for assertions about the physical world, a statement about sensations must entail, or be causally connected with, that assertion. And this is common ground to a sceptic, a phenomenalist and a causal theorist. A sceptic says that to talk of sensations which observers have in seeing, touching and tasting (for instance) a piece of cheese, is not to talk of any reasons for asserting the existence of cheese, for there is never a causal or a necessary connection between the two kinds of talk; sensations, therefore, cannot be reasons for claims about physical items. A phenomenalist, by means of his translations, promotes the different view that to talk of a piece of cheese just is to talk of sensations of a piece of cheese; although the connection between the two kinds of talk is not causal it is, in a special sense, logically necessary. Therefore sensations *can* be reasons for assertions about physical items. And this conclusion, though not for the reasons given by a phenomenalist, is endorsed by a causal theorist who proposes that to talk of touching, tasting or smelling cheese is to talk of the effects of a hidden cause, real cheese.

In all this the rival parties make domestic application of an international principle belonging to the traditional doctrine. If one proposition P is a reason for another proposition Q, then the connection between P and Q must either be causal or logically necessary: a good ground is a ground which inductively supports its conclusion, and a conclusive ground is one from which its conclusion logically follows. The history of the philosophy of perception is largely a record of the major battles and minor tactical exercises fought on the particular terrain circumscribed by this principle. The collapse of the traditional strategy of forging a causal link between perceptions and the physical world left two tenable positions, to dispense with the link altogether, or to make it logically necessary. The time has come to abandon the struggle and remove to a new theatre of operations.

A philosophical theory whose theoretical underpinnings are completely mistaken is a rare thing, and much more common are doctrines raised up by a combination of sound and unsound props. Phenomenalism is one of these. The theory goes well when it expunges, along Berkeley's lines, the canon of a causal connection. It succeeds also, although there is less acknowledgement of the fact, in recognizing an *a priori* connection between the classes of statements with which it deals. Yet it becomes untenable by its claim that this connection must be one of logical necessity. It would seem, therefore, that the thesis of an *a priori* connection is no less tenable; it would seem that the impossibility of a demonstrative connection between statements about sensations and statements about the physical world has a consequence the impossibility of the connection being *a priori*. Is there any justification for supposing that this is true? Of course, it is usually assumed that a connection between a reason and a conclusion could not be *a priori* without being logically necessary, and this is an assumption philosophers have made quite independently of whether they support phenomenalism, or some other position, even scepticism. It is, if the arguments in Chapter 3 are correct, an erroneous assumption. It is not impossible that there should be connections between reasons and conclusions which are neither necessary nor contingent.

Now this clearly has a bearing on the problem of the relationship between statements about sensations and statements about the physical world. For it provides an alternative to the defective deductivist account that is different from the equally defective inductivist account, and different again from the no-connection thesis of scepticism. If a statement a person makes about what *seems* to him to be so can be *a priori* a reason for a statement about what *is* in fact so, without entailing that statement, this effectively dismisses the original need for the introduction of a phenomenalist's translations; it answers the twin demands that the connection be causal or logically necessary, by denying it could be either, without denying that sensations can be reasons.

It is common sense that a person is entitled to say a tomato is red if he sees that it is red when he looks at it. It is a philosophical truth that 'This looks red to me', understood as a statement about sensations, does not entail and is not causally connected with the conclusion 'This is red'. But it is a philosophers' fiction that on this account a person who says 'This looks red to me' has not given a *reason* for saying 'This is red'. For a person who says a tomato looks red to him is giving a reason which necessarily counts in favour of its being red, if it does at all; but its being red does not necessarily follow from the reason given.

For example, the statement 'The flag looks to me as if it were red' is, independently of any empirical investigation, a reason in favour of saying the flag is red. A person who argues from his sensations of a colour to the existence of a colour is not in the position of one who argues that it has been raining from the observation that the roads are wet, but of one who argues that the roads are wet for the reason that he has observed them and that to him they look wet. A person who concludes that it has been raining can give as a reason that the roads are wet only because there is an empirically established correlation between the two kinds of events, and no correlation of this kind lends support in the first case. Yet it does not follow that the person in the first case has no reason for what he says. Although the person who says that the roads are wet because he has sensations of a certain sort is concerned with an *a priori* and not causal connection, and although the connection is not logically necessary, it nevertheless remains true that his sensations give him grounds for saying that the roads are wet; he has *some reason* to say they are wet, even if they are dry as a desert. Similarly, if a person says that a certain flag seems red to him, or to have stripes, it may be false that it is red or has stripes, but not that his sensations count in favour of saying it is red or has stripes. It is easy to misunderstand this thesis and fail to see that, when X is a statement like 'This seems red to me' or 'This seems red to most observers', and Y is a statement like 'This is red', it does not maintain that if X is true then it follows that Y is true, or the converse; what it does maintain is that if X is true then it follows that there is some reason, or some ground, for saying that Y is true. Indeed, this is just the peculiarity of the connection between talk about sensations and talk about physical things which makes phenomenalism so attractive. What gives a person the right to make an assertion about the physical world is ultimately the fact that he has certain sensations and it is only by the occurrence of sensations that the existence of physical things can be verified. But this does not mean that to assert a statement about the physical world is to assert an equivalent statement about sensations. It means that for every statement about the physical world some reason in terms of sensations can be given which counts *a priori* for or against it, even though there is no question of a logical translation. And this is the target a phenomenalist is all along trying to hit.

It is very likely to be held that the relationship of X's counting in favour of Y is a weaker and less respectable or reliable connection than the necessity of entailment. The answer is that the connection is not an inferior stand-in for entailment, but an entirely different connection with an entirely different function. It is a misconception to think that it fails to do the job because it is less than necessary; rather it does the job in cases where a necessary connection necessarily fails, and is a colleague of necessity and not a rival competitor. A philosopher who says that the connection between X and Y, when X is a statement about a person's sensations and Y a statement about the material world, is 'contingent', emphasizes those features of the connection which count against its being necessary, namely that no entailment is present. A philosopher who says that the connection is 'necessary' emphasizes those features which count against its being contingent, namely that a person can know that X is a reason in favour of Y without recourse to empirical investigation. The common denominator of both sides is the mistaken belief that it is impossible for both features to be present in a single connection between X and Y. Once it is realized that to say something about a material object is to say something for which reasons in terms of sensations can be given despite the absence of a necessary connection, we are in a better position to assess the weakness and the strength of, first, a sceptic's belief that no reasons can be given because no reasons that could be given necessitate the conclusions desired; and, secondly, a phenomenalist's belief that reasons can be given because the connection between reasons and conclusion is necessary. Both demands are superfluous. It is not a corollary of the concept of 'X being a reason for Y' that Y must be a logical consequence of X if the relation between them is not contingent.

However the recognition that non-necessary though non-contingent connections between statements about sensations and statements about physical objects are possible falls short of providing an adequate solution to the problems raised by a sceptic. What it does is to remove a main obstacle standing in the way of a solution. Its inadequacy lies in the fact that the problems it dispels are not peculiar to scepticism about

the material world, and are likely to appear whenever a person reflects
on the character of the connections between reasons and conclusions.
For example, the thesis expounded here is helpful in explaining the
connection between evidence and verdict in a court of law. A verdict of
negligence is neither a demonstrative nor a causal inference from the
evidence before the jury. What happens is that the evidence logically
counts in favour of, or against, a particular verdict without entailing
it, and it is the function of the jury to determine by deliberation the
degree to which the allegation of negligence is supported by the evidence which they have. It is tempting, therefore, to allow this comparison to clear away puzzles when it is used as an explanation of the
connections between statements about sensations and statements about
material things. But the parallel seems stronger than it is; and does not
take into account that the connection between the evidence of sensations and a verdict about material things is importantly different from
that between evidence and verdict in a court of law, and different also
from the non-necessary yet non-contingent connection between, for
instance, 'having a nose' and 'being a face'. For there is no inclination
in these cases to say that a subjective reason is being advanced for an
objective conclusion; there is no passage from what *seems* so to what
is so. In these cases the reasons and conclusions are statements of the
same logical type, whereas a sceptic's attack takes place when the
reasons offered are of a different type from the conclusion adduced.
And it is this difference which prevents the view of *a priori* connections
set out here from being an adequate solution to the sceptical puzzle,
even though this view points to a solution by making it possible for us
to dispense with the requirement that the connection must be logically
necessary or causal. However the removal of this requirement is not
enough. A philosopher may allow that there can be *a priori* non-
necessary connections between reasons in terms of sensations and
conclusions about the material world but because of the difference in
verification between them still remain doubtful whether *knowledge* of
such conclusions is possible. His doubt, as we shall see, is needless.

4. *'What the sceptic means could not be wrong'*

One of the objects of this exercise has been to show that the truths of scepticism about the material world are compatible with the truths of common sense. When Wittgenstein remarked that what the sceptic *means* is right, he was underlining just this point. So far from being incompatible with common sense, we could not have knowledge of the material world if a sceptic's discoveries *were* false; for a sceptic has disclosed that in the verification of statements about material things certain logical features are necessarily present. It remains to be seen what these features are and why they are no grounds for doubt.

Underlying the expression of sceptical doubt is a pattern of reasoning that can be set out this way. *i.* We believe that statements of a certain sort M, statements about 'material things' or 'physical objects', are often true and can be known to be true; *ii.* the only evidence for asserting a statement of sort M is the evidence of our immediate sensations, expressed in terms of statements of sort S; and *iii.* any statement of sort M is in every case justified by an inference from statements of sort S. The argument goes, since *ii* and *iii* are true, are the beliefs and claims to knowledge mentioned in *i* ever justified? A sceptic claims they are not.

In the first place his reason is that the inference is not causal: statements about material things are not derivable by induction from the data of sense-impressions on which we must rely as evidence. In proposing this a sceptic does not mean to discredit inductive inference on every occasion of its use, but to impress us with the fact that, although inductive inferences are legitimate in so far as they proceed from premises about sensations to conclusions about sensations, or from premises about material things to conclusions about material things, they are unwarranted in cases where the premises consist of the one type of statement and the conclusions of the other. For it is claimed that, given the condition that the data on which a person must rely for verifying a conclusion about a material thing necessarily consists only of his immediate sense-experiences, an inductive inference to that conclusion would be unverifiable. And this claim could not have been false.

Nor, he argues, is the inference a logical demonstration. Some caution is needed here, for a sceptic's argument may give the impression that he is asserting only that statements about material things are not logically necessary statements; however, as in Russell's argument about dreaming, this is not the main objection. A sceptic is making a stronger claim than that propositions about the material world do not have logical certainty; the main point is that statement M does not follow logically from any statement of the immediate sensory data which are the grounds for its assertion, and that the negation of M is not incompatible with any such statement. A sceptic is not concerned merely with the difference between a logically necessary proposition and a contingent proposition, but with the logical differences between two types of contingent propositions in a case where those of the one type are derived from those of the other. The question at issue is the character of this derivation.

The contention that it is not demonstrative rests on two basic arguments put forward by a sceptic. The first (the 'incompleteness' argument) claims that only an infinite number of statements describing single observations would completely specify all the conceivable reasons in favour of, or against, a statement about the material world. No observer could therefore have *every* reason that could be had for asserting any such statement; the reasons which any observer could give to support or reject it are always incomplete. The second (the 'independence' argument) maintains that premises descriptive of sensations, whether of infinite length or not, are always logically independent of any conclusion about material things. The first argument claims that there is necessarily no *end* to the reasons that could be given, and the second claims that there is a necessary *difference* between the reasons that could be given and the conclusions drawn from them.

The main support for the incompleteness argument is provided by varieties of the so-called 'argument from illusion'. To take the elliptical penny case as an example: a sceptic points out that a penny may look elliptical to observer A, circular to observer B and different again to observer C; since there are an infinite number of possible positions of observation, and since each observation is relevant to verify a statement made about the penny, there is an infinite amount of relevant evidence. Moreover, any particular person who makes a statement about the penny on the grounds of his own immediate observations could not also do this on the grounds of the immediate observations other people could make, and yet these can be no less relevant than his own. Again, the argument may appeal to cases where a person is convinced that what he sees is a penny but finds on further investigation that he was mistaken; although it is conceivable that further observations might continue to support any verdict reached at the time, it is also conceivable that they might go against it. These examples, drawn from an immense stock of possible cases, have the specific function in a sceptic's argument of illustrating and supporting the *a priori* judgement that no person could have *all* the reason for asserting a statement about the material world which conceivably could be had by anyone at any time or place; that however much the data of one's own sensations give one a right to assert a statement about a material thing, it remains true that other possible data could have a bearing on the verification of that statement; there always remain tests which have not been carried out. A sceptic is calling our attention to the infinity of possibilities involved in its verification by remarking something that could not have been otherwise: that no one could have all the reasons that could *conceivably* count for or against a statement about the material world.

The argument may take a different turn, yet still revealing a necessary truth as a result. A sceptical philosopher may argue that even from his sensations at the moment, together with a knowledge of the sensations of himself and anyone else for all time, a person still could not derive a proposition about the material world from such a premise. This is to say that from no set of statements, even an infinite set, about the immediate experience of any person or persons, can a proposition about the material world follow. In this case, a sceptic is not basing his argument on the inevitable lack of an infinity of reasons, as before, but on the logical gap between premise and conclusion. A sceptic is warning against a mistake, which a phenomenalist makes, of disregarding a difference in verification between the statements comprising the premises and those comprising the conclusion. If a conclusion about material things is a logical consequence of a premise about sensations, then that premise must contain at least one statement having the verificational characteristic of the type of statement to be deduced; but if this happens the inference is circular and if it does not happen the inference is invalid. A sceptic is underwriting the point that because of the nonidentity of their verificational features the denial of a statement about material objects is logically consistent with the assertion of any statement, or set of statements, about sensations. What his arguments show is that there is no *demonstrative* connection between them; and this, too, could not have been false.

Are these meta-characteristics which a sceptic discloses adequate reasons to conclude that no one has knowledge of the material world? The answer is no. When we look at the basis of a sceptic's scepticism we find no proposition with which it is possible to disagree. His 'scepticism' is a platitude in paradoxical dress. The platitude is the logical truth that no one could have every conceivable reason for accepting or rejecting a statement about the material world, and that no such statement could follow by deduction or by induction from any sets of statements about sensations. The paradox is the assertion that, therefore, we cannot *know* any statements about material things to be true; or that we can speak of 'having knowledge' only if what is impossible were possible. The kind of real or perfect 'knowledge' which a sceptic requires is thus necessarily unobtainable. But knowledge at the price a sceptic demands is not knowledge at all. A person who tells us, for instance, like Moore, that he knows he is seated at a table, says nothing incompatible with the logical platitudes which form a sceptic's premises; he therefore says nothing incompatible with the paradox which forms a sceptic's conclusion. It does not, as a sceptic thinks, *follow* that our ordinary claims to know are false. There is no contradiction in asserting that a sceptic's premises are logically true *and* that his conclusion that no one has knowledge of material things is a matter of fact false. By assenting to the necessary basis of scepticism we do not thereby assent to its paradoxical results.

If we choose, we can say that what a sceptic means by his scepticism is necessarily true. Or we can say that in the sense in which a philosophical sceptic uses the words 'No one knows such a thing as that there is a book on the table', or 'No one has knowledge of any material objects', they express disguised logical truths, although these words are ordinarily used to express propositions which even if false might have been true, and even if true might have been false. And these propositions are, as we know, often true. So far from its being correct that what we have believed to be knowledge of things in the material world is not knowledge because statements about them have those features which a sceptic mentions, we *could not* have that knowledge of them we do have *unless* these features were present. The menace of scepticism vanishes into an *a priori* insight into the verificational logic of statements about the material world.

7

Scepticism in Ethics

1. *Foreword*

The problems of ethical philosophy provide a congenial environment for philosophical scepticism. The moral philosopher's task is not to issue ethical judgements but to give some account of their justification and it is here that scepticism takes root. Not surprisingly, the arguments which philosophers have deployed against the possibility of justifying ethical statements are revealingly similar to those brought against the justification of statements of fact. There are differences, of course; but the similarities are so marked that a philosopher who has philosophical doubts about ethical statements, and none concerning statements about physical objects, is curiously inconsistent. For the main-line sceptical arguments that apply to the one apply equally to the other. Yet ethical statements are often treated as unique members of a remote province to be contrasted with statements of fact, and not being found empirically testable, cognitive or descriptive, come off unfavourably.

The whole of philosophical ethics is not bounded by the limited though central problem of justification discussed here. Nevertheless writers on ethics have returned again and again to the question of justifying and rationally supporting ethical judgements. The solution is elusive partly because the problem is usually treated as if it were proprietary to ethical philosophy, when it is not. The issues are epistemological, if a label is needed, and only accidentally concerned with the subject of ethics. This chapter will show that the traditional arguments of ethical scepticism are little different from the philosophical apparatus that leads to doubt in other departments of knowledge, and that scepticism in ethics arises from the methodical application of the standard dogmas sketched earlier on. Indeed, ethics is one of the easier targets.

2. *Opening moves in ethics*

In the popular sense of the word it is the business of ethics to tell us our duties, to advise on the rightness of actions and to decide between conflicting moral views. And if this is also the proper occupation of philosophical ethics it is obvious that philosophers have fallen down on the job. The adumbrations of modern moral philosophers are notably deficient in the ethical consolation and advice appropriately issuing from the tracts of a moralist. Yet this is neither an oversight nor a mistake.

The sure sign of a moral philosopher, as opposed to a moralist, is his preoccupation with the *justification* of ethical judgements and decisions, however simple or complicated and trivial or serious they happen to be. To decide whether the piratical actions of a Bluebeard are wicked is not a challenging ethical problem; yet it is a challenging philosophical problem to explain how the obvious moral decision could be rationally supported. From the point of view of an ethical philosopher the seriousness or the silliness of an ethical problem is an irrelevant consideration, since both serious and silly ethical problems contain the same philosophically important puzzles. A philosopher's solution with regard to an ethical triviality applies equally to an ethical profundity. To ask whether any ethical judgement could be verified, whether any dispute about the application of an ethical predicate could be settled, whether reasons could be given for judgements of value, or whether there is any test by which their truth or falsehood could be determined, is to ask these things of *all* ethical judgements and disputes, not only those of moral importance. And there is no need, since the results of his philosophizing apply equally to an ethical judgement and its negation, for a philosopher to take sides in an ethical dispute. His conclusion is logically neutral, and thus independent of the verdict of a moralist.

The question, then, of chief importance in ethical philosophy, is whether an ethical judgement can be rationally justified. If the answer is yes, then the appropriate procedure must be explained; if no, then one must account for the position of moral judgements. How is this question to be answered?

i. A possible move is to appeal to an ethical principle from which, together with a statement of the circumstances at issue, one can deduce an ethical conclusion. Given the information that the Knave of Hearts stole the tarts and the principle that stealing is wrong, the appropriate conclusion follows. But there is an obvious problem about the major premise even if there is none about the argument's validity. Why should the premise be accepted? It is no answer to say that the principle is the consequence of a further valid argument, even if this is true; a procedure of deductive escalation involving successively higher principles results in the problem of justifying a particular ethical con-clusion being exchanged for the (perhaps even more difficult) problem of justifying a general ethical principle. Of course, one might put an end to the matter by insisting that an ethical argument ultimately rests on some undefended maxim. But this is an endorsement of ethical scepticism, not a solution. Or it might be argued that the principle is analytic and in some sense true by definition. This will not do either. A look at the prominent ethical principles proposed by moralists and philosophers discloses that their negations are not self-contradictory. And the reason for this is that the ethical principle to which final appeal is to be made will always be sensitive to possible counter instances. Perhaps, then, it is possible to overcome this handicap by continually revising the principle to accommodate exceptions brought against it. The flaw in this answer is that it is incorrect to speak of 'revising' the principle; for a principle is not expanded or revised when a counter-case is produced, but is rejected. To 'defend' the principle that anyone who steals does wrong by altering it in the light of con-trary instances is to abandon, not to rescue it, while admitting some new and different principle in its place. The decisive objection to justification by appeal to ethical principles is this: although one propo-sition may be defended by deriving it from another, and that other from a further one, the final proposition must be defended in a different way. Since the question at issue is how this could be done, the appeal to principles is no solution.

ii. Perhaps the most common way of supporting an ethical judge-ment is to appeal directly to the circumstances of what happened. For example. A certain man went down from Jerusalem and fell among thieves; a Levite saw him and passed him by; then a Samaritan saw him, bound up his wounds, brought him to an inn and took care of him, giving him money when he left. Suppose that this narrative is elaborated in all its details and a complete account of the incident is presented. Someone who believes that the Samaritan's act was better than the Levite's might, when asked to support his belief, simply describe the incident; he might say it is *obvious* that the Samaritan did what was right, while the Levite failed in his duty.

Philosophers will at once recognize the text-book issues now at stake. Can the judgement about the Samaritan be justified? The standard case, from which it appears to follow that it cannot, goes in the following way. Two people hear the story of the Samaritan, each knows as much about the circumstances as the other; in Hume's words they are 'acquainted, beforehand, with all the objects and all their relations to one another ... no new fact to be ascertained, no new relation to be discovered'. Yet one of them (we suppose) says that the Samaritan's action was better than the Levite's action, and the other says it was not. They agree about the facts of the case and disagree in their ethical assessments. This situation (which can occur *outside* ethics, as we have seen) is the traditional springboard for a number of stereotyped philosophical exercises.

First of all, neither disputant could support his conclusion by inductive inference. To take a case, a person may argue by induction from the sight of shoes showing beneath the curtains to the conclusion that someone is hiding behind them; and there is a short way of deciding the matter by looking behind them. The observations which would confirm 'there are shoes' must be different from those which would confirm 'there is a person'; an essential feature of the inference is a passage from observed to unobserved data. But this feature is missing when one draws an ethical conclusion from the narrative record of what happened. In the case of the Samaritan, no observations beyond those that would confirm what the Samaritan did are needed to decide that what he did was right, or that his action was (or was not) better than the Levite's. Each of the rival ethical conclusions is, so to speak, read off the same description.

It is just this peculiarity that, secondly, makes it seem as if a deductive inference might be appropriate. Yet there are inevitable snags here too. The ethical conclusions of both disputants cannot be correct for the one denies what the other asserts. Although their ethical conclusions are incompatible with each other, neither is logically incompatible with the statement of the facts of the situation, so neither could be a logical consequence of that statement. It is not self-contradictory to describe the event and deny that the Samaritan's action was better, or to deny that the Levite's was better. If there is a connection between the description of the incident and the ethical judgement it cannot be a deductive one.

By eliminating the possibility of justifying ethical conclusions by deductive or causal inference the ground is prepared for what appears to be the only acceptable answer: that ethical judgements, insofar as they are incapable of being justified in either way, cannot be justified at all. The position seems to be that they have no truth values and are not even propositions, but are emotive expressions, or that they have only a prescriptive and commendatory function.

iii. One must reckon also with a person who says that he reaches an ethical conclusion by the agency of an ethical intuition, and allows that although some ethical judgements are unquestionably true no rational argument can be given to establish their truth. Ingeniously, the intuitionist view enables a person to claim that ethical assessments can be unimpeachably correct and also that they cannot be justified by deductive, inductive, or any other form of reasoning. But there are limits even to ingenuity. Intuitionism is a theory likely to be adopted when philosophical argument forces a person into a corner against his better judgement. The intuitionist wishes to avoid the paradoxical air of saying, for example, that it is neither true nor false that Hitler had a worse character than St Francis, and wishes to avoid also the apparent mistake of saying that conclusive argument can be given even when the standard defences break down. This shows at once the consistency and the inconsistency of his thesis with ethical doctrines of the Humean genus. It is no accident that this straddling position had Moore's endorsement, for it is in line with his remark, perhaps the best summary of the bones of intuitionism, that he can know propositions which he cannot prove to be true. Understandably intuitionism has drawn heavy philosophical fire although much of it has been wasted, no doubt, on fanciful claims about the existence of special mental faculties and occult access to the Good. And these are embarrassing items which an intuitionist can afford to drop. When stripped of its inessentials ethical intuitionism leaves the problem just where it was at the start. For

I

the philosophical puzzles of ethics become most perplexing when one is required to show how reasons can be given for ethical judgements that are unquestionably correct, and it is exactly this which intuitionism refuses to do.

3. *Is there a special problem about ethical justification?*

As a result of the failure of these opening moves to provide rational support for ethical claims, we are once more saddled with the problem of how p can be a reason for q if p does not entail q and if q is not causally inferred from p, on occasions when we believe, and act as if, p *is* a reason for q. The set-piece philosophical response is to salvage ethical statements by endowing them with one of the acceptable methods of justification, usually by claiming that they can be deduced from statements of fact; or to reject them as truth-bearing propositions and assign them some other idiosyncratic function. The traditional dogmas sketched in the first chapter are responsible for the direction of each reply. But it is not enough to argue that, since these dogmas collapse, there is no necessity of drawing either of these conclusions in ethics.

There is another factor to be considered, the belief that there is a unique philosophical problem about the justification of ethical statements; one which, it is thought, is peculiar to the statements of ethics, not being also a problem for non-ethical statements. There is a tendency to suppose that there is something unique about judgements of value which has the consequence of their being difficult, if not impossible, to verify. Most often they are contrasted with statements of fact. Thus, there is supposed to be a particular puzzle about the verification of statements of value which is different from any puzzle about the verification of statements of fact. This appears in the invidious comparison drawn between (as they are presented) puzzle-free statements like 'He stole the tarts' and puzzle-full statements like 'His act was wrong'. The belief is that if the latter statement could only be justified in the manner of the former (hence the demand for a deductive connection) then the problem would be solved. But this solution is philosophically ruled-out, and there appears to remain an especially stubborn problem about supporting ethical judgements.

It will be argued here that there is no special problem about the justification of ethical statements. Of course there are problems specifically concerning ethical statements, namely the problems involved in deciding ethical issues in practice and supporting the decisions made; and these are no more philosophical problems than is the problem of supporting a political decision, or a scientific hypothesis, a problem for a philosopher rather than a politician or a scientist. But there is no *philosophical* problem of justification that is not equally a problem of the justification of an ethical judgement's traditional foil, judgements of fact. One main reason for the survival of ethical theories of the Humean genus is the belief in an illusory special puzzle. The mistake is to suppose that the difficulty of giving reasons for ethical statements is one *peculiar* to ethics, when it happens to be an inter-departmental difficulty shared by other, non-ethical, statements as well.

One of the things contributing to the special-problem view is the well-attested connection between ethical language and emotional responses. Ethical predicates can and do arouse feelings; they can be so used to create, alter and direct people's attitudes or interests, and effectively serve the ends of preachers, agitators and advertising copy writers. Moral exclamations can at times be calculated or unplanned exposures of sentiment; personal opinions are evinced by moral outbursts as well as by public declarations. None of this is in doubt. But does the fact that ethical statements have perhaps an infinite variety of psychological effects, show that there is a special philosophical problem about ascertaining their truth or falsehood? Certainly not. Such emotive consequences are not peculiar to ethical language and are shared by innumerable descriptions of fact, being causal rather than logical properties of the words involved. There may be a noteworthy problem about determining the psychological effects of emotive terms, but this does not mean that there is, or is not, a peculiar logical trouble about giving reasons for moral beliefs. One might as well say that because the mention of the Union Jack occasionally creates a swell of sentiment, there is a special problem to do with verifying statements about Union Jacks; or because the words 'made in Britain' provoke one sort of feeling, and the words 'made in Hong Kong' provoke another sort, there is an unusual puzzle about justifying statements in which these phrases occur. We do not wish to deny that feelings enter into ethical judgements. On the contrary, although a person who judges an action to be wrong may appreciate the arguments of another who declares the judgement to be too severe, whether he alters his judgement in the light of these arguments has much to do with whether there has been a change in his feelings towards the action. But if the role of feelings in ethics has been underestimated by intuitionist philosophers it has been exaggerated by the emotivists. From the fact that feelings are involved it does not follow that evaluative judgements are themselves no more than assertions, or expressions, of such feelings.

Nor is this view encouraged by any connections between 'good' and the concept of approval. The fact that a person says a certain act is good may be a reason to suppose he approves of it; but it is not impossible for a person to have a favourable attitude towards what he knows is wrong, or to disapprove of an act which he acknowledges is right. He does not contradict himself by expressing his disapproval of an act which he admits is good. Some philosophers have wished to incorporate the notions of rightness and approval in such a way that the assertion that something is right is tantamount to the assertion that the speaker approves of it. What has disturbed them is that the connection between these notions seems stronger than a merely causal one. There is no need to make a detour here and consider the extent to which this view is correct, for it suffices to say that even if the connection were not causal this by itself is insufficient to establish that it is logically necessary. And the position remains that it is not.

Ethical judgements also have a detectable likeness to commands to do something. But this fact, like the one above, does nothing to establish the existence of a philosophical problem uniquely concerning the justification of ethical statements. No doubt there are a number of domestic philosophical problems about commands, orders, or instructions, and other varieties of prescriptive language; but it does not follow that there must, therefore, be a separate dilemma about ethical (as opposed to other) justification. In any case, ethical statements are only rarely disguised or barefaced orders to obey. The language of the Ten Commandments is the exception, not the rule, in ethical discourse. The act of a soldier who smothers a grenade with his body to save the lives of this companions might well be said to be good, but it is a travesty of ethics to suppose that to call his act good is to command or prescribe others to do the same in a similar case. Admittedly, to classify ethical statements as prescriptions by no means commits one to the model of the command, for if ethical statements have a resemblance to commands they also resemble instructions. If someone asks 'Which way to the station?' and is told 'Turn right at the light' he is not being *ordered* to do anything at all; his informant need not be trying to get him to do something, perhaps he could not care less, although he might have a qualm about passing on misinformation. The trouble here is that the expressions of commands and instructions overlap. A policeman may command you to turn right at the light, as well as tell you the way by the same phrase; in the first case it is inappropriate to ask whether he is correct and in the second it is perfectly proper. When a person asks 'What ought I to do?' there is no particular reason in favour of saying that he is requesting orders rather than asking for information, or that he is more like the recruit who asks what he must do next than the stranger who has lost his way. The analogy between ethical judgements and commands insufficiently emphasizes the role of an ethical judgement as a means of telling someone what is the case, and exaggerates its role as a means of getting him to act.

However the model of the instruction, though an improvement on that of the command, will not do exactly. To give an instruction is to indicate a solution that has already been worked out, yet ethical advice must be appropriate in new and unexplored cases. When a person faced with an ethical problem asks what he ought to do, he is asking what the right thing to do is in the circumstances, and there may be no question of his following instructions that have been laid down. He might be told, for instance, that the right thing to do is to return the money he has found, and to answer in this way is both to advise him how to proceed and to claim that the action recommended is right. The fact that an action of a certain description has been prescribed leaves it an open question whether that action is right or wrong. Although there is indisputably a philosophical problem about how an answer could be justified, it has yet to be shown that the problem is peculiar to ethics.

The claim that ethical language is prescriptive appears to be more far-reaching than it really is. The model of the prescription is attractive on two counts, first because a prescription seems to be neither true nor false, and secondly because requests for ethical advice are appropriately met by prescribing what to do. The first is of interest and importance only to a philosopher who is already convinced that ethical statements can have no truth-values, and so (to him) the analogy appears to hold. The second is of interest though of little importance to the problem of justifying ethical statements, since a prescriptive reply is an acceptable answer to an ethical question about what ought to be done only insofar as it purports to prescribe an action of a certain sort, namely a right action. And the claim that an action is of that sort could, unless it is shown otherwise on independent grounds, be true or false. The fact that an action is prescribed or recommended has, of itself, no bearing on whether it is possible to justify the action as being good or bad. The philosophical view that ethical statements must be prescriptive statements is a consequence rather than a premise of the doctrine that purely ethical statements are not true or false, have no rational support or are ultimately based on undefended principles.

Suppose it is said that there is a philosophical quandary about ethical justification distinctly different from puzzles about factual justification because ethical statements do not describe any happenings, circumstances and events, and in this fundamental respect differ from statements of fact. Well, there is something wrong here at the start. For it is not a mistake to speak of *describing* a man as having bad habits, wicked desires or a good character nor to speak of describing his moral qualities, perhaps as opposed to his physical characteristics. An action or a testimony can be described as selfish or disingenuous, and to do this is at once to inform and evaluate. Enormously many evaluative judgements are *ordinarily* understood as descriptions. On the other hand, the mutually exclusive classification of 'descriptive' and 'evaluative' words is an eccentric philosophical invention, since 'descriptive' is used as a replacement for 'factual' and to mean, among other things, 'non-evaluative'. To say that ethical statements are not descriptive is, in this use, a way of saying that they are not statements of fact; or perhaps one might say, the philosophical use is such that 'descriptive' could be replaced by 'informative', and if a statement is informative it expresses information capable of being verified in the manner in which a description of a matter of fact could be verified.

In order to preserve the dichotomy in the case of words like 'pretentious', 'lazy' and 'magnanimous', which seem both evaluative and informative, their meaning has been fractured into 'informative' (or 'descriptive', 'cognitive') and 'evaluative' components. Now there is no objection to saying that an expression should convey information as well as evaluate, just as there is none to saying that a statement of the facts e.g. 'His bearing was dignified' may be a compliment. And here the speaker is complimenting with his words, not describing what he saw and, quite separately, making a compliment; there are not two things, the remark and the compliment, but one thing, the complimentary remark. Similarly, when a person says an action is cowardly he is not making two separate judgements, one as to the facts and the other as to their worth. There is a middle ground of statements which incline a speaker to say first 'factual' and then 'evaluative' in attempting to classify them, and while neither is incorrect, neither by itself seems to do. It is not always, or even usually, appropriate to ask 'Is this an evaluative statement, or is it a statement of fact?' There are cases where the answer is clearly 'a statement of fact', others 'a statement of value', and still others where one is more or less at a loss for words; at any rate, at a loss for a straightforward classification into one or the other division as, for instance, in the case of Proust's description of M. Legrandin: 'Tall, with a good figure, a fine, thoughtful face, drooping fair moustaches, a look of disillusionment in his blue eyes, and an almost exaggerated refinement of courtesy'.[1] An inflexible philosophical line between descriptive and evaluative statements cannot be drawn in *every* case. It remains to be seen why this distinction has been given such a sacrosanct place.

The desire to pursue the informative-evaluative division to the point even of saying that a single statement is in some sense split into two elements comes from the conviction that ultimately ethical statements differ in verification from statements of fact, and that there is something special about evaluative justification which has no counterpart in the case of factual statements. For illustration, take the word 'pretentious'. The two-element thesis goes like this: 'If it is informative to say that someone is pretentious then the informative aspect can be verified in one way, namely by consulting the facts; but if it is an

[1] *Swann's Way*, translated by C. K. Scott-Moncrieff, London 1960.

evaluative remark to say that someone is pretentious, the evaluative aspect cannot be verified in this way, if it can be verified at all; although the informative component is established by making observations and is, therefore, factual and descriptive, there is something of a mystery about the way the evaluative element could be established. Not by making observations, nor is it deducible from any descriptions of observations. The answer must be that the evaluative element is not the *sort* of thing to which the notion of justification applies; and this is to say that the line between factual and evaluative elements is that between testable and untestable content.' In all of this the fundamental thought is still the idea that rational justification is possible only for the descriptive element.

The one conspicuous argument behind this dogma trades on the fact, not in itself unusual, that people disagree about ethical matters. Of course, people disagree about matters of fact too; but it is often supposed that there is something philosophically noteworthy about ethical disagreement, as though it were of a distinct and peculiar kind. There are really two issues here.

First, there is the contingent fact that people do disagree about ethical judgements and that occasionally although perhaps less often than philosophers depict, ethical disagreements reach a loggerhead stage where one person simply denies what the other asserts. But it is obvious that even if people *do* disagree, it does not follow that they *must*. The inability of disputants to settle their dispute is not a premise from which it follows that their dispute could not be settled, and the fact that they agree on no answer does not show that no answer is correct. The existence of common disputes and unresolved arguments, or even of chronic quarrels and implacable differences, lends no support to the philosophical thesis that ethical debates are necessarily incapable of resolution.

The second and more important, because more relevant, issue is the peculiarity that ethical disagreement can survive agreement about the circumstances in question and the probable consequences of these circumstances. And this is the point from which philosophers have extracted and elaborated the apparatus yielding the conclusion that reasoning is tied to descriptive statements. Once again, the nucleus is Hume's argument. In this situation it seems no longer relevant for one party to an ethical dispute to support his conclusion by referring to the events which both he and his adversary know and do not dispute, for his opponent may deny that the conclusion follows either deductively or causally from a description of the circumstances, and be correct. Now there is a philosophical problem about how, if at all, in this situation any conclusions could be rationally supported; and this is the main problem of justification in ethics, setting the stage, for example, for the 'solutions' of naturalism, intuitionism, and the emotive-prescriptive cluster. But the belief that this particular predicament is *peculiar* to ethical statements is certainly mistaken. Exactly the same problem can occur when the statement to be justified is not an ethical or an evaluative one. It should be plain by now that a question of fact, no less than a question of ethics, can persist beyond a point where further observations are required to answer it; notable examples are borderline disputes about matters of fact. A statement of fact, like a statement of ethics, can call for deliberation, and the question for both is whether a non-demonstrative reflective procedure can result in rational justification. We have seen that the answer to this (not particularly ethical) question is that it can. The problem of giving reasons for ethical judgements is a special problem about *giving reasons*, not a special problem about ethical judgements.

4. *Ethical naturalism*

The view that there is no unique problem about the justification of ethical statements is likely to be misunderstood as a plea for some form of ethical naturalism. For it looks as if ethical statements are being identified with statements of empirical fact, since the contention is that ultimately statements of both kinds can call for deliberative reasoning. Accordingly it must be insisted upon that this is not the case. The problem of justifying ethical conclusions is traditionally framed to be that of passing from statements of fact to statements of value, or of giving an account of the inference from what actually happens to what ought to happen; the intention is to show how judgements of value are supported or defended by judgements of empirical fact. Thus naturalism appears to commit the sin of logically translating evaluative statements into empirical statements; and it may seem that there is, after all, a peculiarly ethical problem, namely how one manages to do this. As we will see, to represent the issues at stake in just this way distorts the nature of the problem.

The dispute between a naturalist and a non-naturalist coincides with the dispute between those who hold that there can be a logically necessary connection between a statement of the circumstances and an ethical conclusion, and those who hold the contrary. Thus these theories have been regarded as alternative answers to the problem of the position of reason in ethics, for it is thought that if the one is correct then the other must be mistaken. They are more accurately though more obscurely assessed by saying that each of them is in some sense true though both are untenable. As often happens in philosophy when it seems that neither of two opposing views could be correct because each asserts something true which entails the falsehood of the other, the solution is to be found by noticing that there is some third false view common to them both.[1] This maxim applies in this case. Naturalists and (most) non-naturalists have in common the belief that if a statement of the circumstances is to be a reason for an ethical conclusion then a necessary connection is required. Both share the supposition that deducibility is the key to justification so far as purely ethical statements are concerned. A non-naturalist, by rejecting the possibility of a deductive inference, adopts the view that ethical statements are in the end undefended; and it is only by denying this rejection that a naturalist is able to claim that a rational defence is possible. These two rival views can be reconciled only by abandoning their common supposition, since the fact that one statement is not a logical consequence of another does not establish that the one could not be a reason supporting the other. A naturalist is right in his conclusion that ethical statements can be justified. A non-naturalist is right in his premise that ethical statements are not deductively derivable from the reasons given for them. The mistake which they both make is to suppose that the naturalist's conclusion is incompatible with the non-naturalist's premise.

The belief that they are incompatible is largely responsible for the contention that Mill in *Utilitarianism* was attempting to define the

[1] See J. R. Bambrough, 'Universals and Family Resemblances', *Proceedings of the Aristotelian Society*, 1961, p. 217.

word 'good' in terms of a non-ethical predicate. A reading of Mill's text shows that at no point does he expressly propose the equation which has laid him open to the charge of committing the 'naturalistic fallacy' namely that 'good as an end' is to be defined as 'what in fact people desire as an end'. Nor does he in any place say that it is his intention to find a non-ethical equivalent for the word 'good'. Nevertheless it is often said of Mill that this is precisely what he did, even if it was not his explicit intention. Why should this accusation seem so plausible?

To begin with we must look at an argument usually acknowledged to be Mill's both by those who claim that he advanced a definition of 'good' and those who say he did not. It is agreed that Mill stated that people do in fact desire happiness as an end, from which he concluded that happiness is good as an end. Both sides of the dispute agree also that Mill's premise is a contingent statement and, although this is a subsidiary point, a statement whose truth no doubt can be challenged. More important, both agree that Mill's conclusion does not follow logically from this particular premise. And it is clear that Mill himself did not suppose that his argument was logically valid, indeed he has expressly ruled out this claim by maintaining that conclusions about ultimate ends are incapable of deductive proof.

The plausibility of the thesis that Mill did, unwittingly or not, define 'good', becomes apparent in the light of a further claim Mill makes: that his conclusion that happiness is good as an end is one which can be rationally supported, not being merely a product of intuition, and that he, Mill, has given argument in favour of it. The question that immediately arises concerns the kind of argument that Mill must have employed. Supporters of the definist thesis have supposed that if Mill were to justify his conclusion then he must, all along, have reasoned deductively by suppressing a major premise in which 'good as an end' is defined in terms of what people do desire as an end. This seems the only face-saving move that could be made, for the invalidity of the argument without such a premise is obvious; and it must be admitted that the obscurity of Mill's language in places, while not supporting this interpretation, at least does suggest it. The next step on this view is to maintain that although the argument is now valid, the major premise is illegitimate for it defines an ethical term naturalistically, and that this is the major, and fatal, criticism of Mill's theory.

Convincing as it is, the interpretation is unsound. For it is not based on Mill's actual procedure but on the belief that Mill could hardly have been doing anything so philosophically naïve as to infer, without further ado, a conclusion about what is good as an end from a general psychological statement about people's desires. Yet the fact remains that this, in essentials, is exactly what Mill did. It is wide of the mark, therefore, to criticize him for proposing a naturalistic definition of 'good'. The problem which Mill set for himself was to justify an ethical principle without resorting to a deductive procedure that would inevitably involve the use of a naturalistic definition as a major premise. Thus he contended that reasons can be given in favour of ethical conclusions by an argument which, he says, 'cannot be proof in the ordinary and popular meaning of the term' and he adds, 'there is a larger meaning of the word "proof" . . . Considerations may be presented capable of determining the intellect either to give or withhold its assent'. These are, he thinks, 'equivalent to proof'. At the outset of his argument Mill is rightly protesting against a too-restricted conception of ethical justification.

Naturalistic theories have come under heavy critical attack in recent years. However, much of the criticism is less destructive than it seems. One of the standard arguments intended to show that 'good' cannot be defined in terms of non-ethical characteristics is Moore's 'open question' argument, which goes something like this. If someone asserts that *i*. 'good' is equivalent to 'having property p', we can significantly ask *ii*. 'X has p, but is X good?' However, *ii* could not be asked significantly if *i* were correct, for then *ii* would be equivalent to asking *iii*. 'X has property p, but has X property p?' which is absurd and not a significant question; therefore *i* cannot be correct.

As it stands the argument establishes nothing whatever about the possibility or impossibility of *i*. Even though naturalistic equivalences must be rejected, this argument fails to secure their rejection. For example, let us take a case where the equivalence holds, e.g. *a*. 'a pentagon' is equivalent to 'a plane figure having five sides and five angles', and apply the same reasoning. We ask *b*. 'X is a plane figure with five sides and five angles, but is X a pentagon?'; *a* is correct so *b* entails the question *c*. 'X is a plane figure with five sides and five angles, but is X a plane figure with five sides and five angles?', which is absurd and not a significant question. Now there is no inconsistency in saying that *a* is correct, that *b* is a sensible question to which the answer is 'yes' and that *c* is an absurd question. It is perfectly clear that *b* might be asked significantly on a number of occasions, equally clear that *a* expresses a logical equivalence and that if *c* ever were asked it would be unintelligible. Most certainly it does not *follow* from anything in the above argument that *a* is incorrect or that *b* is not a significant question. It might *seem* to follow paradoxically that *a* could not be correct, for the reason that if *b* and *c* are equivalent and *c* is unintelligible then *b* must be unintelligible, together with the fact that *b* is not unintelligible. The paradox is created by an oddity of the connection between *b* and *c*: obviously, in the light of *a* they are logically equivalent; but the fact that two questions are logically equivalent does not mean that they must be equally intelligible. The absurdity of asking 'X is p, but is X p?' derives from questioning what one has already asserted, namely that X is p, and this is both to claim that it is true that X is p and to express a doubt about its truth. But to ask 'X is p, but is X q?' is not to question what one has asserted, for by asserting 'X is p' one implies although does not assert that X is q, if it is true that q is equivalent to p; and thus this question lacks the peculiarity that renders 'X is p, but is X p?' unintelligible even though they are logically equivalent. In Moore's version of the argument it is possible that if 'good' should be equivalent to 'having property p', the question 'X has p, but is X good?' should be significant although the question 'X has p, but has X p?' is absurd.

A second reason said to prohibit, or at any rate to count against, the possibility of naturalistic equivalences has to do with the fact (if it is a fact) that the word 'good' has no exact emotive counterpart; therefore it is supposed that 'good' cannot be defined in terms of words which do not have the same psychological effects. And this is correct, if what is meant by defining the word 'good' is finding some other term that brings about identical emotional responses and if it happens that there is no such term. However this is hardly a refutation of a naturalist's equation, since he is claiming that there is a logically necessary, not a causal, link between the terms. The question of emotive identity (or the lack of it) has no relevance to the question of logical equivalence. No one would think that because the statement 'This is my mother' is proper and what one would say, although 'This is my female parent' is pedantic, rude and not what one would say, and because they are emotively different, that there is no logical equivalence between them. Yet the possibility of a logical equivalence is the point at issue, for a naturalist maintains that there is a set of features which together entail, and are entailed by, a thing being good. And this is not shown to be impossible even if the terms related have completely different emotive characteristics.

In short, the case for ethical naturalism remains undisturbed by these arguments. It may seem that the possibility of deducing ethical conclusions from factual premises is still open and that one might defend an ethical judgement by maintaining that a naturalistic definition is correct. Naturalism seems, once again, to offer an acceptable solution to the problem of ethical justification. Nevertheless a solution of this kind will not do.

For one thing, a naturalist frames the issues in a way that misrepresents the nature of the puzzle. For the difficulty of passing from facts to values does not arise from the particular feature that we are dealing with, on the one hand, an empirical statement, and on the other a statement of ethics. The question to be dealt with is whether a certain ethical term can apply properly to a conceivable case, and although the statement of the circumstances of the case is contingent, its contingency is an unimportant factor in the decision. Just as, for instance, the contingency of the statement that Smith parked his car on a hill and forgot to set his brakes is an unimportant factor in deciding whether the action was careless; although the statement 'Smith was careless' is descriptive, one might correctly say it is evaluative as well. If someone reasons 'She pulled the cat's tail, so she's naughty' this involves an evaluative conclusion and a statement of the situation given as a reason. There is a problem about deciding whether pulling the cat's tail is naughty, just as there is a problem about whether a failure to set the brakes is a careless action, but there is no additional special problem arising from the feature that 'She is naughty' evaluates her action whereas 'She pulled the cat's tail' states what the action was. The problem in these cases is straightforwardly one of applying a predicate on the basis of reflection concerning an action, as for instance when one reasons that a person is a skilful player from the fact that he regularly outmanœuvres his opponents in chess, or when one concludes 'She is tall' from the information that she is six feet six inches high.

It is also true that one might decide whether an action is a piece of carelessness without knowing anything about the actual actions a person performs, and express the situation as 'If Smith parked his car ... etc., then he was careless'. This indicates that it is also an indifferent matter whether the statement of the circumstances is construed as a description of an actual occurrence or merely as a statement describing a possibility. If someone says 'She's naughty because she pulled the cat's tail', that the statement 'She pulled the cat's tail' describes an actual happening is irrelevant to the question whether the action is a case of being naughty. For it could be the case that, even if she did not do it, she would have been naughty if she had done it, and this could have decided independently of the occurrence or non-occurrence of the event. Or, if a person had answered the question 'If she pulled the cat's tail, would she be naughty?' without troubling about whether she did or did not do it, enough would have been done, except for observing the incident, to answer the question of whether she *was* naughty. One may say that in evaluating a situation no special weight need be put on its actual occurrence, since the knowledge that it did or did not occur has no logical relevance to whether the situation is a possible instance of a particular ethical concept. This is immediately obvious when one considers that cases from moralists' paradigms to novelists' episodes are judged evaluatively without considering whether they actually took place, and indeed the philosophical practice of inventing ethical examples simply underlines the point. What is of interest is whether the actions narrated in the examples and episodes are such that they could be described and justified as, let us say, good or bad actions, or actions which ought or ought not to be done, irrespective of their occurrence. The problem of giving reasons for ethical conclusions is not in essentials a problem of the logical relationships between factual and evaluative statements, but a problem about the relationship between an ethical concept and the possible circumstances of its application. The question is whether a case is a possible case of K, where K is an ethical predicate.

The 'fact-value' distinction dissolves into the distinction between a concept and its criteria. When one makes a decision to apply an ethical term to a set of circumstances, one is claiming that the circumstances are such as to be a reason for its application. A claim of this kind is not peculiar to ethics for if, in a non-ethical case, the circumstances are that an object has six sides and twelve angles, then this is a reason to call it a cube. But the comparison does not hold in one important respect: there is a necessary connection between 'being a cube' and 'having six sides and twelve angles' whereas the type of connection to be found in ethical cases is comparable to that obtaining, for example, between 'parking on a hill without setting the brakes' and 'being careless'. The term 'careless' is not applied for the reason that it is entailed by the statement of the circumstances, for it is not entailed by them; rather, the circumstances count *a priori* in favour of its application, if they do so at all. The connection here is neither causal nor logically necessary, and this is also true in the case of ethical predicates. To say that X is good is to commit oneself to the claim that there is some reason to say that X is good, but not to the claim that X possesses certain features from which this can be deduced. When a person gives reasons for saying that the Samaritan was good by reciting a description of the circumstances he is not putting forward premises from which his conclusion logically follows. What he is doing is to cite an example of what he claims to be a good action. And this is a deliberative issue that might, like other non-ethical deliberative issues, be settled by rational argument.

One cannot apply the word 'good' to just *any* action or circumstance, just as one cannot apply the words 'intelligent' or 'shrewd' without distinguishing between different actions and different circumstances. To suppose they apply indifferently to different instances is absurd. Nevertheless philosophers have sometimes believed that it is possible for a person to use the word 'good' to refer to whatever situation he pleases, or rather to whatever one that pleases him, and that any action could be counted as a good action. And they have thought, at bottom, that this is permissible simply because a person is neither inductively nor deductively constrained to apply the word to a specific type of case; and once this constraint is eliminated they have thought that there is no possibility of a reasoned decision. However the elimination of these methods of support is not *ipso facto* the elimination of rational support. What circumstances, then, *are* reasons for saying that something is good? This question *is* peculiar to ethics and perhaps the most difficult one of all, though not one that a philosopher need answer: for it is a question of ethics, not ethical philosophy. One of the jobs of philosophical ethics is to show that a person who attempts an answer to this question can have the consolation of knowing that the answer he reaches could be right.

8

Philosophical Method

1. *Reasoning about reasoning*

It is the business of philosophers to mind other people's arguments. The study of physical and mental phenomena, of right and wrong, or of the past or future, is not a part of philosophical practice; these provinces are reserved for physicists and psychologists, moralists and historians. Of interest to a philosopher are the verificational characteristics of statements, questions and disputes which these (and other) studies generate: he is a meta-commentator about first order thinking. To philosophize is to reason about reasoning. This proposition naturally encourages departmental partitioning: the philosophy of science investigates the reasoning of scientists; the philosophy of mathematics the reasoning of mathematicians; the philosophy of psychology the reasoning of psychologists; the philosophy of theology the reasoning of theologians; and so on. Cutting across these partitions is the philosophy, or the theory, of knowledge.

Knowledge is anybody's affair. It does not name an occupation or a calling and there are no specialists in knowledge as there are in aerodynamics or art. There is not a philosophy of knowledge as there is a philosophy of physics; to treat the philosophy of knowledge as on a par with the philosophy of mathematics or psychology, differing only in subject matter, is to be guilty of a serious mis-allocation. There is no proper or professional activity called 'knowledge' as there are proper and professional activities called 'physics' and 'mathematics'. The competence of Plato and Aristotle to philosophize about knowledge is not diminished by the discoveries of Newton, Darwin or Einstein, and their philosophical reflections are neither more nor less fruitful for the two thousand years between them and contemporary science. The theory of knowledge seems, and is, an especially 'philosophical' branch of philosophy, transcending empirical discoveries and professional advances. Yet it deals with exactly the same *philosophical* problems as the philosophy of physics, mathematics, or psychology, when stripped of their non-philosophical specialist uniforms. For the theory of knowledge is a purely *a priori* investigation of the possible types and varieties of reasoning; and reasoning, like knowledge, is not the monopoly of any particular company of reasoners at any particular time. It is a commodity common to every investigation of any problem at any time. On these grounds the philosophy of knowledge is largely taken up with the reasoning of the non-specialist plain man or the specialist in his off-duty thinking. In this book the target has been the reasoning of the specialist in philosophy in his professional moments. The aim has been to give some account of the nature of this reasoning and of philosophical knowledge.

When Newton theorized about the falling apple he was reflecting on things that happen, and his theory is correct or incorrect, appropriate or not, depending upon the facts. There is a difference in excellence, complexity and scope, but not in verification, between the inferences of Newton and those of Sherlock Holmes. Unlike Newton and Holmes, a philosopher's theorizing is concerned with the logical character of reasoning about the facts rather than with the facts themselves. His questions are meta-questions, questions about questions often about matters of fact.

For example. A person may ask whether the height of the Average Constable is six feet. Another person may ask whether the sum of the heights of all constables divided by their number is six feet. A third person may ask whether the first and second persons asked the same or different questions. We can give a right answer to this third question without giving a right answer to the other two; we can know the answer to the third and not know the answer to the first or second. It is impossible to answer the first two by reflection alone and irrelevant in answering the third to investigate empirically the heights of the individual constables: their mode of verification is necessarily different. Philosophical questions are in an analogous position. Sometimes this has been expressed by saying that philosophical questions are 'perennial' or 'timeless'; or expressed by the remark that they are second-order questions and that the investigations they launch are logically independent of the results of empirical inquiries. However there is nothing in this to separate questions of philosophy from questions of mathematics and formal logic, since both are requests for reflection of a certain sort.

Yet philosophical arguments are not formal demonstrations. There are no philosophical axioms, theorems or postulates and a noteworthy feature of philosophical reasoning is the absence of a Euclidian Q.E.D. A philosopher's reasoning is not dismissed solely on the grounds of its difference from a mathematical proof.

These characteristics have given rise to a chronic self-consciousness among philosophers about the nature and methods of philosophical investigation. One standard move, documented in the first chapter of this book, is to suppose that puzzlement about the position of philosophical method can be overcome by locating the reasoning of philosophers within territories ordinarily assigned to non-philosophical disciplines. Philosophy is thus classified as a kind of science, a department of logic, or a linguistic activity issuing verbal recommendations; and the particular sin is the idea that philosophy can be *sui generis*. The source of the dogma is obvious at once. The proposition that there can be no such thing as distinctively philosophical reasoning is based on the assumption that legitimate reasoning is found only in the sciences and in the formal disciplines of mathematics and logic.

Philosophers who draw a parallel between their own procedures and those of scientists often have in mind that philosophical arguments are grounded in particular concrete instances. Philosophical statements are supported by favourable examples and rejected by counter-cases; the technique is appropriate in psychology or physics, and won the approval of Hume. If the view is old it is not old-fashioned, for Professor Ayer in his Inaugural Lecture 'Philosophy and Language' takes a fresh look at philosophical method and the scene he now describes contrasts sharply with his own earlier account. Much of it would not read strangely to Hume. The aim, he says, 'is to see the facts for what they are'; philosophers have argued by the presentation of particular cases and particular counter-cases and this is 'chiefly a matter of the meticulous inspection of a certain range of facts . . . In this respect the procedure followed in philosophy is like that of the natural sciences'.[1]

[1] A. J. Ayer, *Philosophy and Language*, Oxford 1960.

These remarks leave unclear how like and how different from science Ayer conceives philosophy to be. They are equivocal on an important point brought out by his criticism of Wittgenstein. When in the *Investigation* Wittgenstein describes examples of 'reading' he is said not to be engaged in a grammatical investigation and not to be calling our notice to the multiplicity of verbal usage: 'We are asked rather to consider what actually happens when, for example, someone reads a newspaper'. Wittgenstein's examples 'can be taken as showing that what a dictionary might represent as one particular use of the verb 'to read' is in fact a family of uses; but again this would put the emphasis in the wrong place. What is being brought to our attention is the variety of the phenomena in which reading of this sort may consist'. The procedure is not linguistic but an effort 'to see the phenomena as they really are'.

A case can be made for saying that emphasis on its linguistic aspects has distorted Wittgenstein's principal accomplishment, but surely it is wrong to represent Wittgenstein as considering what *actually happens* in cases of 'reading'. The examples he gives describe mainly fictional or imaginary incidents and are not records of what does, or tends to, occur. Wittgenstein himself understood their nature: 'We are not doing natural science; nor yet natural history – since we can also invent fictitious natural history for our purposes'. The examples he mentions are not used as instances to support an empirical generalization. But if they do not record events, then what function have examples of this kind? The answer is that they direct our attention to conceptual possibilities. By reviewing conceivable situations and pointing out, let us say, that some overlooked cases are also examples of 'reading', Wittgenstein is trying to break the hold of an over-simple picture of what 'reading' consists. Whether an instance offered is, or is not, a specimen of 'reading' is an *a priori* deliberative question. In order to discredit the idea that philosophical procedure is, in some sense, a special inquiry to do with linguistic usage, Ayer has succumbed to the temptation to say it must be concerned with, not words, but the phenomena to which words refer. The tendency here, once again, is to place philosophy within the province of empirical investigation.

One may underestimate the value of the picture that Hume and (latterly) Ayer have put forward. On the credit side is Hume's insistence on the role of particular instances which he correctly believed to be the bedrock of philosophical reasoning. And Ayer has ventilated an atmosphere of excessive generality by emphasizing the philosophical use of concrete cases. What has not been made plain is that the use of possible cases signals an *a priori* procedure. It is a contingent matter that philosophers sometimes appeal to examples of things that have actually happened, to recorded incidents, events and situations. It is a non-contingent matter that they must appeal to *examples* and that the actuality of an example is a philosophically irrelevant feature. We may easily and mistakenly suppose that the necessity of giving examples to justify philosophical conclusions entails a stronger likeness between philosophical and scientific methods than there is. To say that philosophy proceeds by the comparison and consideration of particular instances is, most certainly, *not* to say, that philosophy is a branch of science.

If the analogy with science breaks down as an explanation of philosophical method the popular alternative is to re-position philosophy within the province of deductive logic. This too is unsatisfactory, but its rejection leaves the (apparently) awkward conclusion that philosophical arguments are entirely reflective even if they are not formally valid. Or, as Dr Waismann remarks, 'Philosophic arguments are not deductive; therefore they are not rigorous; and therefore they don't prove anything'.[1] This view has an unfortunate consequence, for one might wish to abandon the idea that philosophical arguments are *a priori* if the claim that they are carries with it the rejection of philosophical proof. There is a conflict here between the inclination to think that philosophical proof is possible, and the inclination to think that such proof could not be deductive.

Dr Waismann is right in his premise that philosophical arguments are not logical demonstrations. Much less secure is his conclusion that they are not rigorous, for a rigorous argument can be given even if no deductive steps are invoked. An example striking in its simplicity is McTaggart's argument that a cause need not be like its effect: 'Causes do not necessarily resemble their effects. Happiness in A does not resemble the misery it may cause to the envious B. An angry man does not resemble a slammed door. A ray of sunshine does not resemble a

[1] 'How I see Philosophy', *Logical Positivism*, ed. A. J. Ayer, p. 365.

faded watercolour'.[1] Although rigorous and decisive, McTaggart's argument is untypical. For it consists in directly bringing particular cases to support a philosophical conclusion and is stripped bare of surrounding elucidatory discussion. More typical are arguments of the kind found in Plato and Aristotle, Berkeley and Hume or Ryle and Wittgenstein, where examples are set in a context of discussion and elaboration. Wittgenstein's discussion of 'family resemblances' is one such instance and Hume's discussion of causal connections is another; they have in common with McTaggart's reasoning the operative feature that the discussions and conclusions which emerge are backed up by the examples employed. In both, the final justificatory appeal is the reflective consideration of particular instances. Dr Waismann would agree. 'What do you find', he asks 'in reading Ryle or Wittgenstein? Lots of examples with little or no logical bone in between . . . The real strength lies in the examples.' No appeal is made to premises, canons or axioms, and this explains why Dr Waismann is reluctant to use the word 'proof' in connection with philosophical arguments. He says forthrightly 'proofs require premises', showing that he believes it to be a necessary condition of a proof that its conclusion follows (deductively) from some premises; since philosophical arguments do not fulfil this condition they are not proofs. Of course they are not deductive proofs, and if deduction is a model of proof to which all arguments ought to conform, then Dr Waismann is right. But it is just this supposition which is questionable.

If Dr Waismann's conclusion that 'No philosopher has ever proved anything' is paradoxical and less than satisfactory, the reasons for asserting it are logically impeccable. For Waismann's paradox that philosophers' proofs *could not* be proofs has a logical point, comparable to Hume's claim that there is no reason to suppose that past experience is a guide to the future, a paradoxical way of stating that conclusions about the future necessarily cannot be deduced from premises about the past and present. To say that philosophical arguments prove nothing is an unconventional way of stating that necessarily they are not deductive arguments, that a *philosophical* conclusion is necessarily not justified by demonstrative reasoning. Waisman's scepticism signals a logical truth. However, from this truism it does not follow that a

[1] *Some Dogmas of Religion*, p. 89.

person who speaks of a philosopher as having 'proved a conclusion' or 'given a proof' is thereby mistaken or is, in some sense, using these words incorrectly.

If the analogy with deductive reasoning fails as an explanation of philosophical method valuable and fruitful parallels still remain. The tendency to represent philosophy as a department of logic is an antidote to the opposite tendency to regard it as a branch of empirical science. But the cure is as regrettable as the disease, for the dissimilarities between philosophy and science are revealed at the expense of exaggerating the similarities between philosophy and logic. Philosophers find themselves shuttling between these polar positions because each position pin-points a characteristic feature of philosophical reasoning: there is a likeness to science in that philosophers' arguments are based on a scrutiny of particular instances, and a likeness to logic in that this scrutiny is non-contingent and reflective. Yet one may notice these differences and still present an inadequate picture by representing philosophy as being, in some imprecisely specified sense, a linguistic investigation. This answer is an attractive *general* explanation of the puzzling and frequent conflict between philosophical claims and common sense. It emphasizes that this conflict is *unlike* conflicts between rival empirical conjectures.

This latter point is central to an understanding of the persuasiveness of the linguistic model. If a philosopher says that nobody knows that other people are conscious, a listener can reply 'But you and I are conscious, we both know this, so you are mistaken'. He is correct in saying the philosopher is mistaken in so far as the evidence supporting his reply is logically appropriate to discredit the proposition ordinarily expressed by the words 'Nobody knows that other people are conscious'. If the philosopher insists that he has not been shown to be mistaken, and refuses to acknowledge the destructive consequences even of the best evidence that can be brought against him, then his contention is, to say the least, eccentric. The natural question to ask is how this eccentric claim can be explained.

Can we say that he is not asserting an empirical proposition? If we say this we must meet Moore's objection that while the reasons a philosopher gives for his conclusion may not consist of empirical statements, the conclusion which he rightly or wrongly draws from his reasons –

that nobody knows that other people are conscious – is nevertheless empirical. Could we reply *a*. that the proposition expressed by the words 'Nobody knows that other people are conscious' is not empirical although the form of words would ordinarily express an empirical proposition, for the reason that a philosopher who asserts it does not allow its refutation when presented with facts which would refute it if it were empirical? Could we reply *b*. that a philosopher who concludes 'Nobody knows that other people are conscious' is saying something incompatible with the true empirical assertion 'You and I are conscious, we both know this' and therefore he is asserting falsely at least some matter of fact? If there is reason to say either *a* or *b* is true there is also reason to say each is inadequate. For it is true that 'Nobody knows that other people are conscious' is incompatible with 'You and I are conscious, we both know this' so *a* seems false. But it is also true that the philosophical conclusion 'Nobody knows that other people are conscious' is asserted on entirely *reflective* grounds, and this is suggested by *a* although concealed by *b*. The puzzle to be dealt with concerns the position of this and similar philosophical claims which despite their falsehood seem on reflection reasonable to assert. It is not to be solved by empirical investigation or the employment of formal logical techniques, and is typical of the kind of puzzles to which Wittgenstein turned in his investigation of the nature of philosophical conflicts.

2. *Wittgenstein*

In the *Enquiry* Hume argued that there is no new fact to be ascertained once all the circumstances of the case are laid before us; nothing is hidden to be discovered by further investigation. A comparison with Wittgenstein is striking: 'Philosophy simply puts everything before us, and neither explains nor deduces anything. Since everything lies open to view there is nothing to explain. For what is hidden, for example, is of no interest to us'; 'The problems are solved not by giving new information but by arranging what we have always known'. It is Wittgenstein's intention to reveal the nature of philosophical puzzles by exposing their source. Wittgenstein does not draw Hume's conclusions. He turns his back on the belief that philosophy is a kind of science and warns us against just this step which Hume takes; the tendency to ask and answer questions in the way science does 'leads the philosopher into complete darkness'. Nor does he think that philosophy is logical analysis, and forcefully argues against his own earlier estimation of its role. But if Wittgenstein's conclusions were radically different from Hume's he did not altogether avoid making a typically Humean move in casting about for an alternative place for philosophy. Wittgenstein's reasoning (e.g. 'It is not new facts about time which we want to know. All the facts that concern us lie open before us. But it is the use of the substantive "time" which mystifies us', *The Blue Book*, p. 6) appears to parallel Hume's move from the premise that the facts are all before us to the conclusion that what remains is a matter for the sentiments; with the difference that, in Wittgenstein's case, what remains is a problem to do with the use of words. In the *Blue Book* he says that philosophical puzzlement arises because of a dissatisfaction with a verbal notation: a philosophical conclusion has the character of a linguistic proposal. In the *Investigations* the specific charge that philosophical conclusions are verbal recommendations is not made, yet they are still products of a special kind of perplexity having its origins in language. Being neither science nor logic, he asserts 'our investigation is therefore a grammatical one'. This kind of investigation is conducted 'by clearing misunderstandings away. Misunderstandings concerning the uses of words, caused, among other things, by certain analogies between the forms of expression in different regions of language'. Rejecting the conventional alternatives he was drawn to conclude that 'we may not advance any kind of theory. There must not be anything hypothetical in our considerations' and 'it can never be our job to reduce anything to anything'; that 'We must do away with all *explanation*, and description alone must take its place'; 'Philosophy really *is* "purely descriptive".' This description, he says referring to his own philosophical technique, 'gets its light – i.e. its purpose – from the philosophical problems'. A philosophical problem is based on a linguistic misunderstanding, a 'grammatical illusion' standing in need of correction. A philosophical question is a muddle felt as a question: 'What we are destroying is nothing but houses of cards and we are clearing up the ground of language on which they stand.'[1]

Wittgenstein's remarks about the position of philosophy are vivid,

---

[1] *Philosophical Investigations*, sections 126, 109, 118; *The Blue Book*, p. 18.

forceful and suggestive. Their exact interpretation is difficult, and if one were to try to say, precisely, what they mean, the loss of their immediate effect is unavoidable: their striking, pointed economy and rich metaphorical expression vividly suggest new tracks of thought in a way that no exegesis however scrupulous could achieve. There is a risk in taking them at their face value; yet the risk must be taken, if only to throw light on Wittgenstein's procedure. A scrutiny of his own philosophical achievement discloses an inadequacy, even a danger, in this characterization of philosophy, since the impression that he is engaged primarily in an imprecisely defined inquiry into language – a rough impression his remarks give – conceals what he actually does. Wittgenstein shows us more than ways in which words may confuse. If he draws attention to verbal usages, this is only part of an effort to pull down old misunderstandings and open new conceptions; if he 'clears up the ground of language' he also alters traditional *habits* of philosophical thinking; he consistently introduces unsuspected possibilities and relationships; he points out new directions to follow. And this is not, in any ordinary sense, a linguistic operation. It is something else. A more reliable clue to his accomplishment is his remark, 'I have changed his *way of looking at things*'.[1]

We can get the feel of Wittgenstein's procedure by looking at it somewhat in this way. Often we resort to a comparison to explain a puzzling situation and instruct a person to look, or think, of something as *like*, or as if it were, something else. Suppose a child is puzzled about why the water in the familiar streams he sees always moves in the same direction and why it moves at all. We might tell him to think of it as water running off the roof of a house or flowing down an inclined driveway, to think of the land through which the stream flows as being sloped like the roof or driveway. He will notice at once that the woods and fields of the surrounding landscape are not steeply pitched like the roof and that there are dissimilarities between the landscape and the driveway. Yet this comparison may be enough for him to see for himself the explanation that eluded him; he may go on to comprehend why it is that there are quiet pools, lakes and bogs, as well as torrents and waterfalls. Later on, suppose he questions us about why we speak of electric currents. We tell him to think of electricity in a wire as like

[1] *Philosophical Investigations*, 144.

the flow of water in a pipe. This may immediately give him a grasp of the operation of the switches, plugs and flexes he finds in his house. But he is likely, on reflection, to be puzzled: why then, he asks, do electric currents flow uphill? The comparisons which so easily removed his puzzlement now create new confusion; we must explain to him that analogies which make things understandable in one situation may not be straight away applicable to another: that differences are as important as similarities, and that the picture of a current in a stream does not in *all* its ramifications do justice to the idea of a current in a wire. The operation of correcting this confusion can be more difficult, more complex and demanding of skill, than that of giving the original simple explanations. Often it is made difficult by the fact that the language we ordinarily and correctly use to describe a situation (e.g. when one speaks of 'electric currents') suggests a *view* of that situation which creates philosophical puzzlement.

To take an instance. Wittgenstein remarks that the idea of a 'process' carries with it a particular conceptual picture that commits us to looking at processes in a certain way, e.g. we grasp how one goes on to learn things about mechanical processes by further investigation.[1] Mental processes seem in an analogous position and naturally one is puzzled when, guided by the concept of a physical process, one tries to understand the mind in terms of this picture; the question 'How is it *possible* to learn about another person's mental processes?' becomes acute, for it seems impossible. One may therefore be driven to deny their hidden operation by denying that such 'processes' exist and adopt a behaviourist picture of the situation. But this succeeds only in exchanging a new puzzle for the old one. What has happened, Wittgenstein writes, is that we have been misled by a *comparison* and suppose from the start that mental and physical processes are similar in a way in which they are not. In re-positioning these concepts Wittgenstein is attempting to replace (and not merely get rid of) an inadequate view of the likenesses and differences between them by an adequate and correct one. The emphasis here is not on describing ordinary language but on telling or showing us something new. Wittgenstein does not merely *cite* linguistic usages but *points out* overlooked conceptual connections. In his arguments there is surprisingly little documentary

[1] *Philosophical Investigations*, 308.

appeal to standard forms of speech; there is, instead, constant reference
to examples of particular, ordinary and unusual, sometimes incon-
gruous *situations*. The mistakes to which he refers are not like the mistake of a person who confuses (say) 'ingenious' with 'ingenuous', and
not like that of a foreigner who doubts that participles can act as
adjectives in an English sentence. They are like the failure of grasp
shown by a person who knows the language yet does not see in full
the affinities and differences between, to take one of Wittgenstein's
examples, a railway ticket, a railway station and a railway law, and so
finds himself philosophically puzzled. Stuart Hampshire in his review
of Ryle's *Concept of Mind* notices that the 'two-worlds' myth is a picture that appears in the forms of common speech only because it first
strikes one as a compelling and natural way of presenting the situation.
If the metaphor does injustice it is not because of a linguistic oversight
but because of a failure to appreciate the ways in which it at once
explains and misleads. This is a failure of thought and recognition, and
the kind of deficiency which Wittgenstein has frequently made good.

Wittgenstein sometimes began discussions with the words 'We have
the idea that . . .' – for example, that the mind is like a ghostly person
shut up in a house whose activities are known only from seeing what
goes on outside it. The *naturalness* of thinking of the mind as a spirit
in a house or a pilot in a ship, and its constant historical occurrence in
philosophical and non-philosophical writing, is an indication that the
comparison is not wholly incorrect. There *is* an affinity and the model
does tell us something about the mind. But there are differences central
and crucial for any adequate account of the mind; on its own, the comparison is misleading. The inadequacy of this *picture* of the mind,
Wittgenstein believes, must be exposed before philosophical problems
about mind can be understood. Again, when Wittgenstein said we have
the idea that the meaning of a word is an object, he was opposing not
only an over-simplified philosophical view but also a picture that the
plain man readily accepts, not from persuasion, but because it seems to
fit in so well with, and to account for, his ordinary verbal practice. In
his attack on essentialist theories of universals Wittgenstein goes
straight to the source of puzzlement. His claim is not merely that this
or that theory of universals is unacceptable, but that behind *all* such
theories lies a persuasive comparison whose acceptance constrains a

philosopher to adopt a specific, and mistaken, course of reasoning: 'The idea of a general concept being a common property of its particular instances . . . is comparable to the idea that *properties* are *ingredients* of the things which have the properties; e.g. that beauty is an ingredient of all beautiful things as alcohol is of beer and wine'.[1] His technique is to show the inadequacy of this compelling analogy by pointing to possible cases where it fails to hold. Wittgenstein's central strategy turns on making clear the defects and limitations, as well as the merits, of just such models or 'pictures' incipient in the way we regard and talk about our experience. He speaks of his job in philosophy as one of assembling reminders for a particular purpose. While this phrase conveys that there may be more in a philosophical problem than meets the eye it insufficiently conveys that there may be more in it than we have ever thought of. His remarks about 'assembling reminders' and solving problems 'not by giving new information, but by arranging what we have always known' are modern, original and novel only as descriptions of a philosophical practice already followed by philosophers from Plato to Descartes, from Locke to Hume and A. J. Ayer. The practice itself is not new; it remained for Wittgenstein to drive it home and in this paradoxical way make explicit what his predecessors had not seen clearly, that philosophy proceeds by deliberation.

Wittgenstein constantly returned to the problem of giving an account of how philosophical procedure could be as deliberative as mathematics and as informative as a scientific investigation. There are signs in his work that the reconciliation is less than successful, for his exposition suggests that if philosophy proceeds by deliberation alone then it can disclose nothing new. When Wittgenstein's statement that all the facts lie open before us is read with the remark that philosophy is purely descriptive and does away with explanation, the tendency is strong to suppose that the function of philosophy is wholly critical and clarificatory; and that, accordingly, the job of a philosopher is no more than remedial. What remains, on this view, is the detection and correction on linguistic confusion. But just as Locke caricatured his own procedure by the picture of the under-labourer, Wittgenstein caricatures his work by the picture of therapeutic treatment. Like all good caricatures they convey a truth at the price of distortion. Witt-

---

[1] *The Blue Book*, p. 17.

genstein saw that the method of getting rid of a philosophical puzzle requires more than the refutation of a philosopher's claim, and that a problem can be dissolved only by explaining *why* it happens to be puzzling. This introduces a new dimension to philosophical criticism; for the job is not merely to understand – and accept or reject – a particular philosophical contention, but to understand and explain the influence of a model or comparison through which a philosopher sees the nature of his problem. It is in his sustained attempt to solve philosophical problems by revealing the origins of philosophical perplexity that the inadequacy of the above interpretation becomes clear. Wittgenstein's own practice runs counter to the claim that philosophy discloses nothing new: recognizing and explaining the reasons for the persistence of a philosophical problem is one form of discovery.

Often, Wittgenstein thinks, the explanation of philosophical puzzlement is to be found in an over-simple notion whose acceptance is encouraged simply by the way we ordinarily speak. For example, he writes that in the expressions 'He is capable of . . .' or 'He can play chess' the verb is used in the present tense, 'suggesting that the phrases are descriptions of states which exist at the moment when we speak'.[1] Again, the picture of remembering as an inner process is both suggested by the language we use to describe remembering and also 'stands in the way of seeing the use of the word as it is'. To break the hold of such suggestions Wittgenstein recommends that we carry out a 'grammatical investigation' consisting of looking, unencumbered by preconceptions, at the variety of cases exhibiting the use of the word. But when we see, in fact, what this comes to, it bears little resemblance to anything that ordinarily might be called an investigation of grammar. As he says, ordinary language is 'all right as it is'; however its correctness is compatible with its power to introduce a specific though inaccurate picture or notion of the affairs referred to. Wittgenstein's point is that the *correct* use of language can be philosophically misleading, e.g. 'A simile that has been absorbed into the forms of our language produces a false appearance, and this disquiets us . . . A *picture* held us captive. And we could not get outside it, for it lay in our language and language seemed to repeat it to us inexorably'.[2] It would

[1] *The Blue Book*, p. 117.
[2] *Philosophical Investigations*, 112, 115.

be a mistake to read Wittgenstein as saying that philosophical problems are always or even usually engendered by errors we make in the
usage of words, or by the diffuseness and inexactness of much of common language; it would, therefore, be equally mistaken to suppose that
one might remove philosophical puzzlement by re-defining ordinary
words with more precision. Rather, the problems are created through
a failure to 'command a clear view' of the complex range of possible
situations to which a word can apply, despite the fact that we make
no mistakes in its usage. One result of such a failure is to fall victim
to an over-simple model, to suppose that a word always functions as it
does in a narrow range of conspicuous cases. What is needed is a full
and complete view, a 'perspicuous representation' which 'produces just
that understanding which consists in "seeing connexions". Hence the
importance of finding and inventing *intermediate cases*'.[1] Wittgenstein
is consistent in saying both that 'philosophy may in no way interfere
with the actual use of language' and that philosophical problems arise
'when language goes on holiday'. The forms of ordinary speech frequently suggest a particular though philosophically misleading way of
looking at a problem; and by adopting the suggested point of view a
philosopher sees a situation as being different from how it actually is,
which creates puzzlement when the philosophical requirement to
which one is committed by the adopted view clashes with both common sense and common usage ('But *this* isn't how it is!' – we say. 'Yet
this is how it has to *be*!' *Investigations*, 112). In turn, this preconceived
view conceals the rich variety of cases that need to be appreciated in
order to free oneself from its influence. The solution is to make plain,
by the presentation of particular instances, just how misleading the
picture is, and how it comes to be adopted. Throughout the emphasis
is on changing a person's course of reflection. It is understandable,
though a pity, that Wittgenstein's work should be so often included
under the popular misnomer of 'linguistic philosophy'. What is distinctive, perhaps revolutionary, in his philosophy has little to do with
verbal problems as such; but lies in the originality of his deliberate
attempt to show that the source of philosophical puzzlement is found,
not in the language a philosopher uses, but in philosophical habits of
thinking.

[1] *Philosophical Investigations*, 122.

3. *John Wisdom*

In 'Philosophical Perplexity' Professor Wisdom remarked that a philosophical answer is really a verbal recommendation. No doubt he would not put the matter in just this way today, and there is a hint even in that article that this claim is not so straightforward as it seems. Although he said 'Say which you like' of rival philosophical conclusions he added the warning 'but be careful', and to be careful is to hear out the case, to describe tooth and nail the issues on both sides. The slogan 'Say which you like' had little of the effect it might have had if it were taken as the literal truth. For it might have been understood as a suggestion to stop listening to philosophical argument, or to any argument which has neither the finality of deduction nor the likelihood of induction. Despite the slogan, Wisdom himself insisted that philosophical disputes must be heard. But to what point? The answer was left obscure.

The point that was missed is that in philosophical controversies rival parties are trying to *gain an understanding* of that which they are talking about. Like juries in the courts it is not only a question of a decision but also a question of knowledge and ignorance. This point can be missed by a failure to appreciate the nature of the process that is employed in discussing and concluding reflective issues. By conventional standards the process is eccentric and informal. What needed to be done was to recognize that this eccentricity does not exclude philosophical debate as a means of reaching the truth. In part what prevented this recognition was the inclination of both Wisdom and Wittgenstein to fasten on examples favourable to the recommendations theory; the idea was to encourage philosophers to agree that it was a question of the choice of a word by comparing philosophical questions with questions like 'Is a tomato a fruit or vegetable?' How successful this was can be glimpsed from G. A. Paul's remark that, in a particular philosophical conflict, rival answers can perhaps be decided 'by tossing a coin'.[1] Besides their triviality questions of this sort, in which there is as much reason to give one answer as another, mislead precisely because, in most cases, either answer will do. Borderline cases of this

[1] 'Is there a Problem about Sense-Data?', *Logic and Language* (1st series), ed. Flew, p. 113.

L

paradigm kind obscured what was happening in other cases which though borderline were not trivial, like cases in the courts, and so concealed what was happening in philosophical cases. The importance of the difference between them had not been struck home. What is this difference? Wisdom explains by an example:

> Suppose now that someone is trying on a hat. She is studying it in a mirror. There's a pause and then a friend says 'My dear, the Taj Mahal'. Instantly the look of indecision leaves the face in the mirror. All along she has known there was something wrong with the hat, now she sees what it is. And all this happens in spite of the fact that the hat could be seen perfectly clearly and completely before the words 'Taj Mahal' were uttered.[1]

Even though each person sees what the other sees, one of them simply by pointing out a feature of the situation alters and adds to an apprehension of the case. In this instance the remark about the hat is more than a suggestion about what to call it. It is a new comparison and a new discovery. The simplicity of Wisdom's move can hide its far-reaching implications. At once we may see connections between this case and other comparable occasions on which talk and thought finish with a knowledge of the circumstances not present at the start, in spite of the fact that no further investigation is made.

Among these occasions are philosophical discussions. A philosopher's conclusion need no longer be seen as a disguised notational choice, but as the end of an argument in which he seeks to explain a problem comparable in its genuineness to a problem in science or logic, and to be solved by non-deductive reflection alone.

Wisdom's diagnosis of the basis of doubts about other minds is a case in point and complements Wittgenstein's treatment. Like Wittgenstein, he is interested in exposing the source of philosophical puzzlement. But the emphasis is different. For Wisdom it is less a matter of pointing to a philosophical mistake than of disclosing a discovery that has been improperly brought to light in terms of a philosophical paradox; the source of the problem is a feature to do with the verification of statements which has been incorrectly expressed, and its correct expression will add to knowledge. Where Wittgenstein says

[1] *Philosophy and Psycho-Analysis*, p. 248.

that philosophical problems should completely disappear, Wisdom re-marks that that to which they refer could not have been false. A scep-tic's doubts about mind are unconventional expressions of a 'logical asymmetry' necessary and peculiar to the verification of statements about mind. If, as a sceptic claims, A knows that B is angry only if it is true that A knows this *as B does* and *in the way B alone does*, then A never does know, never could know, that B is angry. But this is not what 'knowing that B is angry' means; and not what is conveyed on particular occasions when one person speaks conventionally of know-ing how another feels. Although a sceptic may speak as if A stands in ignorance of the feelings of B, this is not ignorance of any ordinary sort but an 'ignorance' which is logically irremediable. In spite of a sceptic's exaggerated claim, Wisdom argues that a sceptic has noticed something that might never have been noticed by one who has had no more than normal doubts about mind. In short, a sceptic's doubt is philosophic-ally valuable since it draws attention to the logically inevitable contrast between *i.* questions to which A's feelings of a certain sort give A *more* authority to answer than do similar feelings give to B, and *ii.* questions to which A's feelings of a certain sort give A *as much* authority to answer as do similar feelings give to B. The former are questions about mind, the latter are not. Moreover, this *logical* difference to which a sceptic paradoxically points does not demonstrate that the ordinary and conventional things one says about the feelings of others are false, or true; to discover their truth or falsehood is to proceed as one ordinarily does proceed when questions about another person's mind arise. The difficulty in opposing a sceptic is not merely one of refuting his con-clusion, but of getting him—and others—to recognize the nature of his doubt and the logical truth it expresses.

Wisdom is inclined to take as the starting point of a discussion philosophical problems expressed in the form of paradoxical utterances characteristic of traditional scepticism. At first this approach may seem too one-sided. Might not the issues be clarified at the start by phrasing the problem as a question of analysis or of the usage of words? The answer is, not always. When a problem is thus reformulated it is natural to ask whether the analysis or statement about usage is correct, and this can deflect interest from the more important question of *why* an analysis or an examination of usage is felt to be necessary in the first place. The merit of what Wisdom calls the 'paradoxical form' of the problem is its very absurdity, which makes us suspect that there is something at issue over and above the truth or falsehood of a sceptic's remarks. And this suspicion is correct.

To take an example. In 'A Defence of Common Sense' Moore says, 'The strange thing is that philosophers should have been able to hold sincerely, as part of their philosophical creed, propositions inconsistent with what they themselves *knew* to be true'. It is evident, Moore goes on, that philosophers who have held to be true such propositions as 'None of us knows any proposition which asserts the existence of material things' and 'None of us knows any propositions about the existence of other selves, and that they are conscious' *do* know on occasions such propositions as 'Here is a table' and 'That person is conscious'. Characteristically Moore demands a plain answer to a plain question: 'When he (Russell) says that no human being has ever known such things, I think he implies that I haven't, and that therefore I am wrong in thinking that I have. And the question I want to discuss is simply this: Was he right in thinking that I haven't, or am I right in thinking that I have?'[1] Although Moore's paradox reveals the common sense absurdity of a sceptic's claim, it conceals that a sceptic's literally false remark is the result of a partial insight into the verificational features of the type of statement with which he is concerned. By adopting this technique in which he opposes something which is strictly false with something strictly true, Moore has framed the problem in such a way that the issues at stake are obscured rather than clarified by the extreme clarity and simplicity of his question. Strictly, Moore is right; yet his answer misrepresents the situation, and all the more for being true. This is to say that there can be a gap between a correct answer and what might be called 'seeing the position at issue'. Sometimes a situation can be presented in a false light by a statement which describes that situation correctly. A man who has a watch from which the hands are missing still has a watch, and if someone asked 'Has he a watch, yes or no?' the answer 'Yes' is correct even though no one could tell the time by it. This *true* reply may be of less value in appreciating what is the case than the *false* reply 'No' for it suggests that the watch in question is more like a typical watch than it happens to be. Wisdom

[1] 'Four Forms of Scepticism', *Philosophical Papers*, p. 200.

has spoken of questions like 'Is a watch without hands a watch?' (or 'Can one play chess without the queen?' to which the correct answer is 'Yes') as being *sub-acute* in that they refer neither to typical nor to borderline members of a class. They mislead for often what ordinarily can be said of typical cases can be said also of them without a mistake; the ordinary and correct thing to say conveys no hint of the unordinary situation being talked about. Moore's truthful answer is in a comparable position: it suggests that Russell's doubt is not very different from a typical non-philosophical doubt, that Russell is wrong in the way in which a person who is not a philosophical sceptic might be wrong about a matter of fact.

It comes out of this discussion that there may be more to a philosopher's conclusion than the words he uses ordinarily convey. In order to see the character of philosophical questions and answers Wisdom insists we review their logical history rather than rely on the form of words in which they are expressed. The steps which a philosopher takes to reach his answer are of more interest than the answer itself and a scrutiny of his conclusions must be subordinated to a scrutiny of his argument. We cannot tell what he means simply by paying heed to his results: for the *meaning* of his conclusion lies in the arguments he gives for asserting it, and these arguments are the primary objects of philosophical inspection. In short, to understand a philosopher's conclusion is to understand the reasoning behind it.

Again Wisdom places emphasis on *seeing* what is so, not *saying* what is so, a matter of recognizing and coming to apprehend the logical features which a statement of a certain type must have to be a statement of that type. But attempts to see a philosophical situation properly can be hindered by a misapprehension of the nature of one's own inquiries and of philosophical questions and answers. In consequence Wisdom is concerned with the place of philosophical reasoning itself. It would be a mistake to suppose that he lays down a specific procedure to follow. Although there is no recipe or simple nostrum for the conduct of philosophy, the subject is delineated by certain logical ground rules. Philosophers' questions are not settled, like scientists' questions, by investigating what actually happens, but by 'reviewing the possible' along non-deductive lines. The investigation is, and could only be, reflective. In the tradition of Wittgenstein and Moore, Wisdom's technique is to deal with an abstract puzzle by putting it in concrete terms.[1] If we wish to understand the philosophically puzzling remarks of philosophers we should 'avoid asking them to define their terms, but instead press them to present us with instances of what they refer to contrasted with instances of what they do not refer to, then their pronouncements will no longer appear either as obvious falsehoods or mysterious truths or pretentious nonsense, but as often confusingly presented attempts to bring before our attention certain not fully recognized and yet familiar features of how in the end questions of different types are met.'[2]

How can philosophical procedure be as reflective as a purely logical procedure without being deductive? Wisdom has replied somewhat along the following lines. On some occasions people regard what they see before them as a sign of something further to be seen. On other occasions that which people see before them is not regarded as a sign of anything further to be seen. There is an inclination to think that although in the former case a person can ascertain the truth or false-hood of a statement about what is seen, for one can and indeed must investigate further, in the latter case no additional verification is pos-sible for there is no call for further observation. Consequently, if in this case persons disagree about what is before them, there is an inclination to think that they are no longer engaged in an effort to answer a ques-tion about what it is; rather, their disagreement concerns a matter of verbal usage, or perhaps reflects only a difference in attitude among the persons. One may be tempted to think that the dispute here is not a real dispute since there is no conventional way of settling it. All the while, however, that feature of the situation which encourages this response is the fact that their disagreement about what is before them could not be brought to an end in the way in which it could be in the former case where the settlement involves testing one's expectations. It appears, therefore, that there is no way of bringing the dispute to an end. Wisdom urges that it does not follow from this *difference* in mode of investigation that there is no possibility of coming to a right answer when the circumstances are of the latter sort. He calls attention

[1] See Ch. 4, section 4, of the present book.

[2] 'A Feature of Wittgenstein's Technique', *Aristotelian Society Supplementary Volume*, 1961, p. 13.

to how people in this position, lawyers, accountants, moralists, novelists, among others, do proceed to give reasons for correct answers
despite this feature. The procedure they use may be no more than a
matter of rearranging the data, of presenting them differently; often it
is a matter of drawing comparisons with possibilities not hitherto considered. What has this to do with philosophy? Although philosophers
engaged in debate are not, like lawyers or accountants, attempting to
understand the actual, their efforts are none the less directed towards
answering questions to which the answers are not known; and the procedures they adopt differ from patterns of typical inductive or typical
deductive reasoning. To see that this departure from conventional
procedures of reasoning is not a defect, Wisdom recommends that we
look at occasions of argument outside philosophy, at specimens of reflective reasoning in which non-philosophical issues are resolved, then
move back to specimens of philosophical conflict. To do this is to
reason by comparison; and to carry out comparisons across a full range
of occasions on which people are conducting reflective investigation is
to efface the old, restricting picture of rational argument dominated by
the deductive-inductive model.[1]

John Wisdom's philosophy both criticizes and continues the tradition of classical British epistemology, and in significant respects is
closer to the spirit of Locke, Berkeley and Hume than to the work of
(say) Ryle or Austin. The connection does not lie altogether in his
constant return to the topics of mind and the material world, or to the
fact that he, like them, has made the problems of philosophical scepticism a central issue. The affinity is more diffuse and more important.
In Wisdom's work there is continuing emphasis on philosophical discovery, a desire to reveal what for good reasons is concealed by habits
of talk and thought, to use his words. This same emphasis is uniformly
found in philosophers from Locke to Hume. They have urged us to
notice that things are not quite as we take them to be, that we are
often ignorant of the truth. For all Hume's insistence on philosophy as
an empirical inquiry he never lost sight of the idea that by drawing
upon things one knows the results of philosophy can add to what one
knows. Philosophy, to him, was a source of knowledge. The claim is

[1] See 'The Metamorphosis of Metaphysics', *Proceedings of the British Academy*,
1961, pp. 55-9; and *Philosophy and Psycho-analysis*, pp. 248-54, 264-70.

open to misunderstanding, and Hume himself misunderstood it. Most certainly it would be accepted by Wisdom, and the difference between Wisdom and his traditional predecessors comes out most clearly in its interpretation and reveals what is central in his work.

Index

reasoning, and philosophy, 15,
138–40, 159
the sceptical pattern of, 79, 96,
107, 112, 117
the traditional doctrine of, 1–5,
17, 46, 51, 77, 107, 122, 140
Russell, B. A. W., his sceptical
arguments, 57–9, 85, 91–6,
97, 156–7
his theory of descriptions, 9,
11
on logical principles, 72–3
Ryle, G., 143, 149, 159

scepticism, about other minds,
154–5
about the physical world, 56–9,
79–102, 103–4, 106, 156–7
its basis is logically true,
104, 112–16
and dreaming, 56–7, 91–6
in ethics, 117–22
self-evident, 71
sense-data, 12, 85, 86, 90, 91, 104
Stout, G. F., 82

tautologies, 22–3

universals, 149–50
utilitarianism, 130–2

verification, principle of, 18

Waismann, F., his view of philosophy, 142–4
Wisdom, John, 17, 81 n., 101 n.
on philosophical method, 153–
160
and reasoning by cases, 52,
69–71, 77–8
and the 'verbal recommendations' theory, 10, 12, 14,
153–4
Wittgenstein, L., 40, 75, 101 n.,
112
and the *Tractatus*, 7, 8, 9.
on definitions, 48–9
his use of examples, 141, 143
his view of philosophy, 145–
152, 153, 154